Advance Praise for

ORGANIC WEDDINGS

Organic Weddings is a great guide for those who want to make their wedding a reflection of their lifestyle without compromising the quality of the event. From the initial planning to honeymoon, Michelle covers it all.

— NELL NEWMAN, Cofounder of Newman's Own Organics and author of
The Newman's Own Organics Guide to a Good Life

It's a real art to balance style with ethics, being chic and ecologically-aware ... and very few people can pull it off. One of the exceptions is Michelle Kozin and her information-packed guide to organic weddings is a winner. I'll be recommending it to all of my clients who are brides-to-be!

— DANNY SEO, Editor at Large, *Organic Style*

With her Organic Weddings website and Bridal Registry, Michelle Kozin shows how to marry style and ethics — joyfully.... Most important, she's shown that going green can be outright romantic.

— *Victoria* magazine, February 2003

Michelle Kozin is a genius. She has though of everything. This wonderful book weaves together all the threads necessary to create the sort of wedding everyone dreams of: lots of fun, perfect food, perfect settings, and most importantly, one that proclaims to the world who we are and that we care. We care not simply about today, but for all the tomorrows and not simply about ourselves, but about all people, everywhere.

— AMY DOMINI, Founder and CEO of Domini Social Investments, author of
Socially Responsible Investing: Making a Difference and Making Money

Organic Weddings is my kind of resource — inspiring and practical, and proof (if you still need it) that conscious living is incredibly stylish. Even choosing just one "green" element for your wedding makes a difference, but why stop there when Kozin makes it so easy?

— Peggy Northrop, editor in chief, *Organic Style*

Organic Weddings

Balancing Ecology, Style, and Tradition

MICHELLE KOZIN

NEW SOCIETY PUBLISHERS

Cataloguing in Publication Data:
A catalog record for this publication is available from the National Library of Canada.

Cover design by Diane McIntosh. Cover image ©Derek Photographers.
Book design and layout by Gregory Green.

Printed in Canada.

New Society Publishers acknowledges the support of the Government of Canada through the Book Publishing Industry Development Program (BPIDP) for our publishing activities.

Paperback ISBN: 0-86571-496-7

Inquiries regarding requests to reprint all or part of *Organic Weddings* should be addressed to New Society Publishers at the address below.

To order directly from the publishers, please add $4.50 shipping to the price of the first copy, and $1.00 for each additional copy (plus GST in Canada). Send check or money order to:

New Society Publishers
P.O. Box 189, Gabriola Island, BC V0R 1X0, Canada
1-800-567-6772

New Society Publishers' mission is to publish books that contribute in fundamental ways to building an ecologically sustainable and just society, and to do so with the least possible impact on the environment, in a manner that models this vision. We are committed to doing this not just through education, but through action. We are acting on our commitment to the world's remaining ancient forests by phasing out our paper supply from ancient forests worldwide. This book is one step towards ending global deforestation and climate change. It is printed on acid-free paper that is 30% old growth forest-free (30% post-consumer recycled), processed chlorine free, and printed with vegetable based, low VOC inks. For further information, or to browse our full list of books and purchase securely, visit our website at: www.newsociety.com

NEW SOCIETY PUBLISHERS   www.newsociety.com

To Kyra, for the inspiration;
and to the brides and grooms,
for making a difference.

Contents

Acknowledgments

THIS BOOK WOULD NOT HAVE BEEN POSSIBLE without the hard work and dedication of a number of talented individuals. I owe them all a great deal of thanks for their enthusiasm and assistance with both this book and with the Organic Weddings website.

My immeasurable thanks goes to Alice Hartley for her valuable research, writing, editing, and all-around great work, as well as for a wonderful sense of humor, which kept me laughing. My gratitude also goes to Stacey Petruzella for always being there when there was more to do, and for her excellent feedback. To Tabitha Brown, for always listening, and for her terrific suggestions. To Betsy Roxby, whose talent and generosity first breathed life into the design and creation of Organic Weddings, and for her ongoing assistance in keeping OW's style consistent. To Kristi Wiedemann for her help getting the OW website off the ground. To Mara Engel, Cheryl Roth, Claire Whitcomb and Victoria Scanlan Stefanakos for providing those early, top-notch opportunities that helped spread the word about Organic Weddings. And without a doubt, much appreciation goes to the talented individuals at New Society Publishers for putting Organic Weddings to paper (and post-consumer recycled paper, at that!).

Thanks also to the organic industry leaders I interviewed, for giving their time and sharing their insights: Amy Domini, Barney Feinblum, Kat James, Gary Hirshberg, Nora Pouillon, Dave Smith, Betsy Taylor and Alice Waters. To Hal Brill, Jack A. Brill and Cliff Feigenbaum for their expert advice on socially responsible investing. To Ann Keeler-Evans for her refreshing perspective and important ideas on creating meaningful wedding ceremonies. To Tedd Saunders for a view into the greening of the hospitality industry. To Jennifer Devine Camp for her expertise on gemstones and jewelry. To Carol Schoenenberger for her knowledge of creating healthy, natural homes. Thank you one and all for sharing your wisdom.

I especially want to thank the many brides and grooms who shared their wedding stories and photos, and for their desire to help pioneer the consciousness-raising of an industry that desperately needs it. Without their creativity and enthusiasm, this book would be lacking many excellent resources, helpful advice and wonderful photographs. A big thank you goes to the many talented photographers who generously shared their beautiful photographs for this book. Their amazing images bring the ideas and ideals of Organic Weddings to life. A special thanks goes to Cory Despres, Michael Weschler, and Derek Photographers for their images (see p. 176 for a complete list of photographer credits).

And of course, as always, considerable thanks goes to my family and friends for their continued support, especially to my mother, Kathy, for always digging in to help wherever and whenever needed; to my grandmother, Alison, for her steadfast guidance; and to my daughter, Kyra, for providing the inspiration to make a difference. And finally, my most heartfelt thanks to my husband, Dan, for his encouragement, patience and love.

CHAPTER 1

Why Organic Weddings?

ONCE UPON A TIME, marrying couples striving to live balanced, healthier and more natural lives had to either trailblaze their own conscientious celebrations or set aside their values and fund the wedding industry machine. People were faced with spending many thousands of dollars on events that went against how they lived and shopped every day. Many did not steer their significant wedding budgets toward more thoughtful purchases because the alternatives were either inaccessible or unrefined.

Now, a new approach to wedding planning has taken root. Couples concerned about the environment, human rights and building a sustainable economy will gain knowledge, resources and inspiration from *Organic Weddings*.

> Conservation of land and conservation of people frequently go hand in hand.
> — Eleanor Roosevelt

This book is a comprehensive guide for busy, eco-aware brides and grooms wanting to plan beautiful, meaningful weddings. By choosing items like tree-free and recycled paper for invitations, organic or local ingredients for your menu, eco-friendly flowers, or even favors that help the homeless, your wedding can be a statement of doing good things from beginning to end — without sacrificing style or tradition. From backyards to black tie, a wedding is the perfect opportunity to show family and friends the stylish side of environmental and social responsibility.

ECOLOGY IN THE BALANCE

The Laws of Ecology:
• All things are interconnected.
• Everything goes somewhere.
• There's no such thing as a free lunch.
• Nature bats last.
— Ernest Callenbach

Growing concerns over pollution, fossil fuel dependency, social injustice and disappearing biodiversity are among the many issues driving millions of aware people to choose more balanced lifestyles. For both special event and day-to-day purchases, this book will broaden your knowledge and understanding of how the true costs of your buying habits and lifestyle impact both people and planet. But sustainability doesn't mean sacrifice, you can have the beautiful wedding of your dreams, minimize your impact and achieve your vision.

As more and more people realize the power of their wallets over business behavior, they are making their money matter. Yet, this concept is not about perfection. The world isn't going to change by having a few ecologically perfect people in it. It's going to get better when a groundswell of people find reason to change their consumption habits in countless big and small ways. Act on your power to influence environmental and social issues through every dollar you spend. Whether you are a novice recycler, a dedicated activist or anywhere in between, you can make a difference simply by investing a bit of extra thought into the planning and purchasing decisions you make.

YOUR STYLE, YOUR VALUES

Your wedding is a wonderful opportunity to showcase your style and express your personality. Far from the plastic fairytale offered by the wedding industry machine, thoughtful brides and grooms are planning weddings that are making a difference, without sacrificing style. Beyond your favorite color and musical taste, your personal style is about the values you believe in, the person you are, and who you want to become. Let your celebration be an outward reflection of your inner values and personal style.

A great opportunity lies ahead. In a pleasing and subtle manner, a bride and groom have the opportunity to share their ideas and ideals with their sphere of influence — an average of 150 of their closest friends and family. Besides putting your wedding dollars to work to support good companies, products and services, you can help inspire your guests to incorporate more sustainable choices into their daily lives. Planning a wedding is a magical time. Keep these guidelines in mind as you create your special day:

ECOLOGY

Ecology – The interactions among living beings and their environment.

Urban Ecology – The patterns, networks, balances and cycles of human impacts on nature in areas of concentrated population, like cities.

Social Ecology – The political and social issues contributing to human impacts on the Earth.

Deep Ecology – The spiritual or religious awareness of our relationships to the living world.

(Adapted from *Ecology*, by Ernest Callenbach)

Natural Nuptials

ALICIA AND MARK — JUNE 21
UPSTATE NEW YORK

*H*igh school sweethearts Alicia and Mark were engaged on the winter solstice (also the bride's birthday) and chose the summer solstice as their wedding day. Because they both work on environmental issues within various nonprofit organizations, the couple felt strongly that their wedding should reflect their commitment to the environment.

The couple used all recycled and tree-free papers for their wedding stationery. Their save-the-date cards were printed on 100 percent recycled junk mail paper and recycled denim paper. Their invitations were printed on handmade recycled cotton paper with embedded wildflower seeds. Other printed items, including their wedding program and thank you notes, were made from recycled papers containing hemp and kenaf fibers. "Everyone absolutely loved the save-the-date

cards and many people were so excited about planting the invitation that they planted it *before* the wedding, which left me wondering if they'd know when to be where…" said Alicia.

Alicia and Mark also incorporated many natural elements throughout the ceremony and reception, to represent the beauty of the Finger Lakes Region of Upstate New York. The wedding took place outside in the gardens of Ithaca's historic Rose Inn. The full service dinner for 175 guests featured all local and organic produce, as well as wild Alaskan salmon and organic, free-range duck. Their eye-catching five-tier wedding cake was also 100 percent organic. Because the Finger Lakes Region of Upstate New York is a big wine-producing area, the couple chose a 95 percent organic local white wine, and also served a 100 per-cent certified organic ☞

Natural Nuptials

☞ Bonterra red wine from California. All other beverages served were certified organic as well, including beer, tea and shade grown coffee from a local Fair Trade-certified company. The ceremony music was a string quartet with a full 11-piece band for dancing at the tented reception. "Unfortunately, one unplanned natural element was also included: rain. Luckily, the food was so outstanding and the band was so energizing, that the rain and mud didn't really bother anyone," said Alicia.

The tent poles were decorated with branches and trees that came from nearby land already being cleared for development. The seating card table arrangement was made from an old piece of driftwood from Cayuga Lake (the largest of the Finger Lakes), drilled with five holes to hold cylindrical vases of simple flowers. On the tables, natural rocks from the shores of Cayuga Lake were scattered among the candles and flowers. Instead of just numbers, the tables were each named for a scenic area within the Finger Lakes Region. Mounted black and white photographs illustrated each location so guests could become familiar with vistas from the surrounding area.

The interactive guest book was a big hit. The couple provided a Polaroid camera for guests to take instant photos of themselves, which were then attached to pieces of Dutch money paper (made obsolete due to the conversion to Euros) which celebrated the groom's heritage, and on which guests wrote congratulatory notes to the couple.

For one of the couple's gift registries, they chose to support an individual woman artist who had started her own ceramics business producing hand made dishes. The wedding favors were organic cloth bags, with a custom design by the groom's brother-in-law. "We wanted to give our guests something that they could use over and over again, while at the same time reducing their reliance on disposable bags – made from non-renewable sources," said Mark.

The couple enjoyed a luxurious, yet eco-conscious honeymoon in French Polynesia, where they were entertained by the cultural festivities of the islands and spent time scuba diving, enjoying the beauty of the undersea world. 🐚

1. Appreciate what brings meaning into your life. It might be family, friends or career; or possibly taking a walk along a beach or through a peaceful forest. Maybe you find meaning through your religious or spiritual beliefs or helping a special cause. Whatever it may be, recognize that which fulfills both you and your fiancé(e) so you can incorporate elements into your wedding celebration.

2. Believe in yourself and follow your passions. If you have been drawn to planning an organic wedding, think about what local and global issues are most important to you: water quality? climate change? recycling? human rights?

Whatever it is, making a difference can be a driving force in your wedding planning. Get that aligned and other details will fall into place more easily.

   3. Don't let being ecologically perfect get in the way of doing good. At certain points in your wedding planning journey, you are sure to feel conflicted by the need to negotiate around your environmental and social goals. To find the best solutions, do what you can, where you can, and don't be overwhelmed by the pursuit of perfection. You have already taken a big step towards making a difference by committing any part of your wedding budget to support companies that you believe in.

"

Learning about ecology can change your life... Ecological knowledge brings us face to face with the underlying paradox of our place on Earth today: understanding the marvelous intricacy, variety, and beauty of life give us endless delight, but coupled with this joy comes the pain of seeing how grievously destructive to the web of life are our industrial, agricultural, and personal activities as we now practice them. Fortunately, we do not share this paradox alone. Ecological consciousness is increasingly shared by millions of others.

— Ernest Callenbach, *Ecology*

"

Words of Wisdom

AN INTERVIEW WITH ALICE WATERS, OWNER-CHEF OF CHEZ PANISSE RESTAURANT

*I*n 1971, Alice Waters opened Chez Panisse in Berkeley, California, with a commitment to serving local, seasonal and absolutely fresh ingredients. Over 30 years later, Alice is a recognized advocate of reconnecting agriculture, food and community. Working with a local middle school, she pioneered the Edible Schoolyard Project, which involves children in all aspects of tending, harvesting, cooking and sharing food from a schoolyard garden, while integrating lessons in science, nutrition and stewardship of the land, as well as breathing new life into the school lunch program. Among her other affiliations, Alice is the Executive Director of the Chez Panisse Foundation, an International Governor for Slow Food, and a dean of the French Culinary Institute. She has published eight books and received numerous awards, including the James Beard Humanitarian Award and the Best Restaurant in American award for Chez Panisse from *Gourmet Magazine*.

Organic Weddings: **Who or what shaped your life with respect to the values we see in your company and career?**

Alice Waters: I was certainly shaped by my experience of traveling in France. I went there in 1965, as a junior in college and it changed my life. It was an awakening of my senses to see how people fed themselves. It was fundamentally different. I like to tell a story about a meal I had in Brittany at a small restaurant where the trout was caught in the stream out back and the vegetables were picked from their garden. It was that immediacy about the food — the aliveness of it that was so significant to me. Unfortunately, in the US we live in a 'Fast Food Nation' so many people don't have the opportunity to eat real food like that.

Also important to me was my involvement with free speech and anti-war movements here in Berkeley, California. That experience gave me an awareness of where I was in the world and how I could be part of a community with a sense of values that I hold very dear. In starting the restaurant, my dream was to create a place ☞

Words of Wisdom (contd.)

☞ where people could enjoy meaningful conversation and delicious food. Just the other night, I was sitting at a table here with two friends who were with me when we started. I realized, here I am 30+ years later, doing just what I wanted — debating the politics of the day with cherished friends.

OW: Whether menu planning for a special event or day-to-day, how can couples incorporate their personal values into healthy meals that celebrate and preserve the earth?

AW: It is important that we buy food from people who are taking care of the land and not from those who damage it. Eating and menu planning should be done with regard to the available seasonal, local and organic ingredients. Buying food from farmers' markets supports local people and local communities, and leads us to the best-tasting foods.

Too often, people don't stop to consider the consequences of the decisions that they make in their everyday lives. This approach connects us to our community and helps enrich our everyday lives. But if we don't pay attention, we are inadvertently destroying the planet.

(See Chez Panisse's Seasonal Foods Calendar on p. 159.)

OW: Given the environmental and social challenges of our time, how can businesses make a difference, protect the environment and promote sustainability?

AW: At Chez Panisse we use our buying power. It is a great way to support the environment. We buy from the people who are taking care of the land and farming sustainably — those with honesty and integrity. What we are trying to do is support local small-scale businesses. I've often said that small-scale is human-scale.

OW: Why organic weddings?

AW: A wedding is a symbolic and special moment in one's life. Having an organic wedding can lead you down a very important path and ensures that you are paying attention to those important details. The result will inspire your community and make your celebration even more extraordinary.

In some form or another, we need to be teaching sustainability to every person on the planet.

Hopefully there will come a time when we won't have to say "organic" weddings, because they will all be organic. ☙

KEEPING TRADITIONS AND CREATING PURPOSE

Your "something blue" shouldn't be how you feel about the wedding industry and its glossy fantasy world. If you suspect conventional wedding planning is lacking substance, you're not alone. *Organic Weddings* offers you the crossroads of ecology, style and tradition to help you create a conscientious celebration with purpose. We encourage you to choose ways to maintain time-honored family, spiritual and cultural traditions, and even start a few of your own. The cherished rite of creating a union between two loving people brings family and friends together in a way that no other gathering equals. The community that gathers around you at your wedding is a blessing. Embrace this chance to do good things and to create memories you'll celebrate together through the years.

Enjoy reading through this book, visit our website at <www.organicweddings.com>, contact the companies listed in our online Resources Directory. Find ways to live a life together in greater balance with nature and community. Share the information with others. After your wedding, use this book as a comprehensive reference to live more sustainably and naturally. Above all, start off together on a hopeful note, not just for your own future, but also for our global future. Best wishes for a wonderful marriage and may you live happily ever after in the better world you're helping to create.

WOW — WHY ORGANIC WEDDINGS?

*E*very year in the US, over 2.4 million people get married, fueling a wedding industry estimated at $70 billion per year. (Source: <www.theknot.com>). This provides an enormous opportunity to turn wedding expenditures into ones that support responsible businesses — those committed to helping our environment and social causes.

CHAPTER 2

Planning Calendar and Budget Basics

THE INFORMATION IN THIS CHAPTER will help you focus on making the right decisions, on time. Depending on the length of your engagement, you will have some flexibility as to how quickly you need to finalize your plans.

PLANNING CALENDAR CHECKLIST

We've included page numbers as a quick reference guide to the location in this book where eco-friendly options on certain topics are discussed.

Six to Eighteen Months Before

• Talk to your fiancé(e), as well as all parents, planners, or other hosts about the wedding to help set expectations and understand their priorities.

Find your place
on the planet,
dig in, and take
responsibility
from there.
— Gary Snyder

- Set your wedding date.
  - Check out dates which have meaning to you online at <www.organicweddings.com>.
- Set your budget, including spending caps on each wedding expense, to help prevent going over budget.
- Determine your wedding style:
  - Formal, informal, big, small, evening, morning, traditional, contemporary? Options abound. Your ceremony and reception locations may help you focus on a wedding style (pages 61 and 72).
  - Time of day? Morning and early afternoon events are typically more informal than late afternoon and evening events. This will also help determine what food and drink you will offer your guests.
- Create your guest list and make sure your budget, number of guests and wedding style are all in concert with each other. It is easy to underestimate how costs can add up. Don't get caught up in overspending. If you don't want to shrink your guest list, consider a wedding reception that offers a cost-cutting lighter menu, such as an afternoon tea or a dessert buffet.
- Consider green options for cermonies. Reserve your ceremony location and select an officiant (pages 61-63).
- Consider non-profit facilities and green hotels for your reception. Reserve your reception location (pages 72-73).

"*My* fiancé and I decided to forgo the traditional money-wasting, headache-inducing, detail-stricken wedding. We opted instead for an intimate event for 50 family members and close friends on Captiva Island on the Gulf Coast of Florida. It was so stress-free that we spent the first part of our wedding day at the beach and pool. Our late afternoon beach ceremony — with barefoot bridesmaids and groomsmen in sandals — was perfect. We had our reception at a well-appointed inn, which required no additional decorations, was located next to our ceremony site and was also where our guests stayed! The absence of any transportation and decoration headaches was not only more eco-friendly, it helped our wedding flow effortlessly. After the official festivities, everyone celebrated until the wee hours of the morning at the Inn's cozy bar." — *Ally*

- Choose your caterer. Ask about serving organic and local/seasonal food, recycling, donating leftovers, and so on (pages 74-75).

- Choose special friends and family to be in your wedding party and consider options for their wedding attire (page 27).

- Decide on a bridal gown style, find a gown you love and order, buy or sew it. Look for natural fabrics (pages 25-27).

- If you plan to use the following services at your wedding, begin to gather contact information, make choices and sign contracts. Aside from professionals, consider friends and family who may be skilled in one or more of these fields:

  - Photographers (page 112)
  - Videographers
  - Transportation (page 113)
  - Florists (pages 91-95 and 97)
  - Wedding cake bakers (page 79)
  - Musicians or disc jockeys (pages 70 and 86)
  - Hair and/or makeup stylists (page 35)

- Register for gifts (page 108).

Four to Five Months Before

- Contact your ceremony official to discuss and begin work on details such as readings, vows and music (page 56).

- Choose your tree-free wedding invitation stationery and place order or purchase paper (page 43).

Q&A

I'm torn between supporting local independent businesses and large corporations that offer sustainable products. Any advice?

Independently-owned businesses maintain strong ties to the community and provide an alternative to the homogenizing effects of a corporate-dominated economy. They struggle against the buying power of large corporations, which can often out-compete them on price. On the other hand, large corporate buying power can jump-start markets in everything from organic food and fiber, to recycled paper, and fair-trade coffee. Through tireless campaigning, environmental groups have scored some huge wins — such as getting Home Depot to stop carrying old-growth wood products and pressuring Starbucks to start selling Fair Trade Certified coffee. Ultimately, if nobody buys these environmentally-preferable products, it doesn't do much to back up environmentalists' efforts of persuasion. As in other things, balance is the key. So, support your local independent businesses if you want to see them around next year. However, in certain situations consider giving your support to the big guys who are taking steps in the right direction.

> "*An* environmentally and socially responsible wedding is *not* all or nothing. Organic components, environmentally responsible choices, etc. can be taken individually. Everything is a tradeoff. Don't feel guilty if some of the choices you make are not as socially responsible as others. Most of all, don't give up on incorporating some more sustainable alternatives into your wedding simply because you can't incorporate everything." — *Wendy*

- Make sure you have the accessories to wear with your wedding gown, such as veil, undergarments, jewelry and shoes (pages 27, 39 & 41).

- Order your organic wedding cake from a local bakery if your caterer will not be supplying it (page 79).

- Make decisions on your floral arrangements, bouquets and other decorations. Choose organic, local, silk or other eco-friendly options wherever possible (page 91).

- Confirm all arrangements with other vendors, including rental equipment, if needed.

- Reserve a block of rooms for any out-of-town wedding guests (page 123).

- Finalize your honeymoon plans and book your trip. Find ways to travel with less eco-impact (page 113).

Two to Three Months Before

- Create a schedule of events for your ceremony and print programs on tree-free/recycled paper.

- Create a schedule of events for your reception. A timetable is important for ensuring your reception goes like clockwork. Give a copy of the timetable to your caterer, photographer, videographer and DJ or bandleader.

- Send a playlist to your DJ or discuss music selections with your bandleader. If you are making your own CDs to play at the reception or ceremony, begin working on them (page 86).

- Finalize your eco-gift choices for your attendants and wedding party (pages 101 & 104).

- Mail your tree-free wedding invitations (page 48).

- Determine what needs to be done for getting your marriage license.

- Practice your first dance.

One Month Before

- Catch up on all guest replies not yet received and give your final guest count to the caterer.
- Finalize your seating plan and have place cards and programs made (page 67).
- If you plan to have your hair and makeup done on your wedding day, do a practice run (page 35). However, don't let that lovely look go to waste — schedule something special with your fiancé(e) for later that evening.
- Have your final dress fitting; make sure it is pressed and ready for the big day.
- Confirm any transportation arrangements (page 113).

> "*In* total, the buffet dinner we provided at our wedding cost more than the food we buy at the grocery store all year. Since I carefully consider my purchases when I go shopping, it made sense to incorporate as many organic and locally grown items as possible into our wedding menu. It was a great opportunity to show my friends and family how to support organic and local farms."
>
> — Stacey

One Week Before

- Hold your ceremony rehearsal with all wedding party members (page 58).
- Make sure everyone's outfits are complete and ready for the big day.
- Pack for your honeymoon (page 42) and reconfirm reservations.
- Create a contact list of all vendors and carry it with you, in case you need to call any of them with last-minute issues.
- Be sure groom and groomsmen pick up their formal wear.
- Make sure your marriage license paperwork is ready.

On Your Wedding Day

- Give the rings to the best man if you want him to carry them.
- Bring envelopes of money to tip your wedding vendors for a job well-done. You may also be paying the officiant's fee on your wedding day.
- Assign someone to help with:
    - Making sure the photographer/videographer captures your special family and friends.

- Answering any questions that arise from your vendors.
- Returning any rentals, including tuxedos, after your wedding day.
- Bringing your floral arrangements to a local hospital or nursing home the day after your wedding (page 93).

- Smile, relax and enjoy.

CONSUMPTION DYSFUNCTION

So many decisions. So many things to buy. Feeling caught up in the wedding rush? If so, take a minute to get your eco-savvy feet back on the ground. Remember, the first step to planning an earth-friendly wedding can be choosing not to buy something at all. Don't get spellbound by the wedding industry's notorious promotion of excess. Your dream wedding can become a reality without it. Remember that the wedding industry tends to capitalize on a bride's enthusiasm for planning her special day. Test your knowledge of America's vast consumerism by taking the Center for a New American Dream's Consumption Quiz online at <www.organicweddings.com/quiz>.

BUDGET BASICS

This budget is for your wedding day expenses and does *not* include items such as a bridesmaids' brunch, the rehearsal dinner, or your honeymoon. Be sure to keep those costs in mind when determining your true total budget.

Your total wedding day budget:_____

Ceremony

3 percent of your budget = _____
Includes:

WOW —
WHY ORGANIC WEDDINGS?

*O*ur throw-away culture is heavily impacting our environment. Every product comes from the Earth and must return to it in one form or another. Consider these facts from the Center for a New American Dream:

- America consumes 40% of the world's gasoline and more paper, steel, aluminum, energy, water, and meat per capita than any other society on the planet.
- The average American produces twice as much garbage as the average European.
- Recent scientific estimates indicate that at least four additional planets would be needed if each of the planet's 6 billion inhabitants consumed at the level of the average American.

- Wedding rings
- Marriage license
- Church/synagogue/other ceremony site fees
- Officiant fee

Reception

50 percent of your budget = _____

Includes:

- Site fee
- Catering costs (including tax and tip)
- Bar and beverages

Natural Nuptials

STACEY AND DAN — JUNE 28
MONMOUTH BEACH, NEW JERSEY

Dan and Stacey met in New York City through a mutual friend. After months of dating, they took a weeklong summer vacation to Acadia National Park in Maine. Soon after, Dan and a friend joined Stacey and one of her best friends for the last 100 miles of a 274-mile hike on Vermont's Long Trail. "While I think we fell in

love in Acadia, I think we realized we could work through anything after the Long Trail!" said Stacey. "Two years later Dan proposed to me on the top of Mt. Tom in Massachusetts. I was completely surprised and absolutely thrilled!"

The couple's love of the great outdoors, as well as the bride's career researching environmental effects on public health, guided their eco-conscious wedding choices. All of the papers used for the wedding were tree free and recycled, from their kenaf invitations to their recycled US currency ceremony programs. The bride's gown was an eco-friendly, matte hemp/silk strapless ball gown accented by a band of shiny hemp/silk charmeuse atop the bodice. Stacey's two flower girls also wore hemp/silk dresses, with silk eyelet overlays. For her two bridesmaids, Stacey chose stylish, short dresses to avoid having them buy more typical brides-maid dresses that they would never wear again.

Wanting organic flowers, Stacey and Dan located an organic farmer about 15 miles ☞

Natural Nuptials

☞ away from the wedding site whom they contacted and asked if she would be willing to grow the flowers for their big day. The farmer agreed and in the spring, planted many types of flowers. On the day before the wedding, Stacey, along with her mom, grandmother, aunts, cousin and bridesmaids picked a bounty of organic flowers and brought them back to the hotel to create the arrangements: 14 centerpieces, 9 boutonnieres, 3 bouquets, 3 corsages and 2 baskets for the flower girls to carry!

"The farmer had never grown flowers for a wedding and after a rainy, cold spring I was pretty nervous. But I had an abundance of bright, beautiful flowers — zinnias, snapdragons, lavender, and many others — fresh from being picked the day before and free of chemicals," said Stacey. "I also saved a lot of money by going through a local farmer and felt great that I was able to support the local organic farming community."

The couple chose to be married on the beach at the New Jersey shore, allowing the shoreline and ocean to be the backdrop. Initially, the couple considered some type of decoration to serve as an altar, but they soon decided the beauty of the unadorned, natural ocean view was perfect all by itself.

The reception site was 50 feet away at a beach club, allowing the couple to be eco-savvy while saving money by not renting transportation or making their guests drive to a second location. The couple chose Bonterra organic wines for their reception. The lavish buffet dinner for 112 guests emphasized mostly meat-free choices at the request of the bride, who is a vegetarian. The couple also made sure their photographer was experienced at taking digital photos and asked him to shoot a combination of film and digital formats, due to the environmental advantages of digital.

Stacey and Dan honeymooned in Costa Rica. The couple stayed at a locally owned eco lodge in the cloud forest where they hiked and explored the rainforest. "We chose Costa Rica for its natural beauty and because it was a place where we could hike and take in some local culture," said Dan. "Every place we stayed had green policies, even the airport hotel." 🐾

- Wedding cake
- Transportation/parking
- Renewable energy certificate ($30-$60)

Music

8 percent of your budget = _____

Includes:

- Ceremony
- Cocktail hour
- Reception

Flowers and Decorations

8 percent of your budget = _____

Includes:

- Ceremony site
- Bouquets, boutonnieres, etc
- Non-floral accessories, such as candles
- Reception site, including centerpieces

Attire

10 percent of your budget = _____

Includes:

- Gown
- Headpiece/veil
- Undergarments/lingerie
- Jewelry
- Shoes/wrap/gloves
- Hair and makeup
- Groom's ensemble
- Additional wardrobe needs

Photography

8 percent of your budget = _____

Includes:

- Photography
- Videography
- Portraits, photos, albums

Stationery

4 percent of your budget = _____

Includes:

- Invitations
- Announcements

" *We* prepared and agreed on a mood board before I went to Australia to plan the wedding details. The mood board had pictures, (ripped from magazines, books, pamphlets) quotes, and expressed our feelings about what we wanted the wedding experience to be like. I used this board to make all of the practical decisions, so it kept me on track and confident it would be something we both like even though my fiancé was back in California. Because most of my planning was done quickly, the mood board was invaluable in helping me to make my decisions fast and then to not worry about them once they were made." — *Elise*

Words of Wisdom

AN INTERVIEW WITH AMY DOMINI,
FOUNDER AND CEO,
DOMINI SOCIAL INVESTMENTS

Amy Domini has worked in the investment field for over 20 years and is a pioneer in the field of socially responsible investing. She is credited with debunking the myth that taking social and environmental performance into account leads to lower investment returns. Her groundbreaking work helped clear the way for many other social funds that have sprung up in the past decade. She also founded a research firm to help quantify corporate accountability and is the author of popular investment books, including *Socially Responsible Investing: Making a Difference and Making Money.*

Organic Weddings: Who or what shaped your life with respect to the values we see in your company and career?

Amy Domini: My grandfather helped instill in me two of my main passions: gardening and Wall Street. He grew dahlias, and I was helping him one day when he turned to me and said, "You know, it's *extremely* important that you know the difference between a stock and a bond." I was only 14, but he proceeded to explain the difference. He also taught me to read an annual report. "Start at the back," he would say.

OW: As newlyweds set up their finances together, many would like to fit socially responsible investing into their plans, but are budget-conscious. What are the possibilities for those just getting started?

AD: One basic thing for a couple to think about is where they do their banking. At the Social Funds website <www.socialfunds.com> you can look up community banks and credit unions in your area that are helping to rebuild struggling communities. I think many newlyweds would be surprised to find how small the required minimums are to start investing with your values in socially responsible funds, IRAs, or regular accounts.

OW: Given the environmental and social challenges of our time, how can businesses make a difference, protect the environment and promote sustainability? ☞

Words of Wisdom (contd.)

☞ **AD:** The analogy I like to use comes from the cowboy shows I watched when I was growing up. In almost every episode, there would be a scene where some vulnerable person would be traveling in a stagecoach when something would spook the horses and they would start to stampede. Out of nowhere, Cowboy Bob would ride up, grab the reins, and lead the stagecoach to safety.

Today it's the world's financial institutions that are stampeding out of control, and the rest of us are being dragged behind and heading for disaster. The only Cowboy Bobs that can rescue us are investors — and that's why it's so critically important that more and more individuals and institutions consider social and environmental factors in deciding where to invest their money. Investors are powerful because they stand at the juncture between finance and commerce. At another level, businesses are consumers, too, and have significant purchasing power when it comes to setting up and running their operations. For example, we moved our offices to an historic cast-iron loft building in lower Manhattan. Before we moved, we took a number of steps to make it healthy and sustainable by asking ourselves: What are the social and environmental records of the companies we contract with? How can we maximize the use of recycled materials and minimize toxic materials? How do we maximize energy efficiency?

OW: Why organic weddings?

AD: For most people, throwing a wedding is expensive. You want to have the best possible time, of course, but in the end it feels good if you know that you have also minimized waste and environmental impact and helped support companies whose work you believe in. You might buy organically grown flowers for the ceremony, or serve organic food and fair trade coffee at the reception. Green Mountain Coffee, for example, has a superlative record on corporate social responsibility.

Finally, a wedding is a new beginning, and an opportunity to begin aligning your investments with your values. By setting up a well-balanced portfolio of socially responsible mutual funds — perhaps with the help of cash gifts you may have received — you can not only help ensure your own financial future but help bring about a world that values and supports human dignity and environmental sustainability. 🐾

"*Being* creative and breaking away from the norm is the best way to make your wedding more personal, more memorable, and even less expensive. Much of the cost of a conventional wedding comes from the huge premium vendors charge for wedding-specific items and services. Consider alternatives, such as a creative cake from a local baker instead of a "wedding" cake, or a venue outdoors, such as a backyard or the town green, rather than a conventional wedding reception venue." — *Wendy*

- Thank-you notes
- Postage
- Ceremony programs
- Menu cards, place cards
- Calligraphy

Other Items

9 percent of your budget = _____

(This category can really add up quickly, so be sure to watch your budget.)

Includes:

- Welcome baskets for out-of-towners
- Attendants' and other gifts
- Favors
- Your wedding night accommodations
- Planting/purchasing trees to offset travel-related carbon emissions ($30-$60)

CHAPTER 3

Eco-chic ~ Brides and Beyond

A S THE BIG DAY APPROACHES, the work to be done may seem endless, but planning for your look and style at the wedding is lots of fun, with great eco-friendly options to consider. From finding the right dress to wedding jewelry and more, these eco-chic ideas help to keep your day your own — in both style and substance.

FASHION FUNDAMENTALS

No matter what your style or budget, choosing your wedding ensemble should always be magical and enjoyable. However, much of what the wedding gown industry offers is either mass-market gowns of synthetic fabrics from overseas factories or silk gowns for $2,500 and up. For brides wanting a more conscientious fashion alternative, consider these suggestions:

> "
> Our task must be
> to free ourselves by
> widening our circle
> of compassion to
> embrace all living
> creatures and the
> whole of nature
> and its beauty.
> — Albert Einstein
> "

Reduce reliance on overseas factories where labor practices can be sketchy and petroleum-based synthetic materials abound by choosing to have your gown made by a local bridal seamstress using all natural fabrics such as hemp, silk, organic cotton or Tencel (a wood cellulose fiber from managed tree farms). You could also reduce demand for new gowns by purchasing a discontinued style sample gown or from discounted overstock.

The bride is wearing a vintage eyelet lace dress. Her bridesmaids are all wearing 100% hemp dresses by Ecolution. The flowers are locally grown, organic sunflowers.

Re-use a gown that has already been enjoyed through vintage, consignment, rental or family sources. Purchase a once-worn or sample gown from Brides Against Breast Cancer <www.makingmemories.org>, which donates all the proceeds of their traveling gown sales to help women with breast cancer. In New York City, a non-profit boutique called The Bridal Garden <www.bridalgarden.org>, resells donated designer gowns, many of which have never been worn, at up to 75 percent less than their original retail price. All proceeds help needy

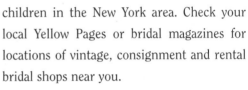

children in the New York area. Check your local Yellow Pages or bridal magazines for locations of vintage, consignment and rental bridal shops near you.

Recycle your gown after the wedding by consigning it at a local store or online auction site. You could also use the yards and yards of beautiful material to create another keepsake item, such as a quilt. If you plan to keep your gown, have it properly cleaned and boxed in acid-free paper so that it will be ready to be worn again by other family members in the years to come.

Styles and Textiles

The style of your gown will help dictate the smaller details. Use natural options to round out your ensemble — for example, silk organza for veils instead of petroleum-based nylon tulle. Headpieces from porcelain, paper, silk or real flowers are a nice touch. If you choose real flowers, be sure to choose hardy ones that will take a day out of water and still look good. For guidelines on choosing a gown style, visit <www.organicweddings.com>. To put your best foot forward with eco-friendly shoes, try Moo Shoes <www.mooshoes.com>, EcoDragon <www.ecodragon.com> and Rawganique <www.rawganique.com>. You can even find eco-friendly wedding accessories. Vintage wedding purses, embroidered shawls, and jewelry make classic accents and are available from antique and vintage shops.

For your bridesmaids, resist the impulse to make them purchase synthetic, cheaply made, overpriced dresses they won't wear for more than six hours. Instead, give your bridesmaids a color and style guideline and let them find something that works for you and that they will wear again. Another option would be to find a fabric you love — maybe a nice print in your wedding colors — and have shawls made. Tell your bridesmaids to wear a solid color dress in a complementary color. You could try to find rentals; they aren't well advertised,

For this casual and colorful wedding, the groom and his men chose 100% organic cotton shirts from Patagonia.

but do exist. If you do end up with dresses your bridesmaids won't be wearing again, donate them to Goodwill, the Salvation Army or the Glass Slipper Project <www.glassslipperproject.org>, a Chicago organization that collects and gives away free formal dresses to high school students unable to purchase their own prom attire.

No matter what your gown style — summer brides (and bridesmaids) be sure to watch those tan lines. Whether you are a sunbather or just enjoy the outdoors, you will not be happy when your wedding photos show that tee-shirt tan in your strapless gown.

Greening the Groom

Grooms and groomsmen benefit from the standard practice of renting tuxes. This makes the most sense, as, for most, a tux isn't an item needed on a regular basis. However, if the men's attire doesn't call for tuxedos, consider buying some natural

fiber clothing, like pants and jackets in hemp, silk blends or wool — and look for low-impact dyes, too. Shirts, both dress and casual, can be found in organic cotton or a hemp/cotton blend. Other options include choosing an ensemble that the men can use again and again, like the ubiquitous khaki and blue blazer combo. Vests, ties and cummerbunds can all be found in natural fabrics like hemp and silk. Visit <www.organicweddings.com> for more ideas.

Think reuse! The classic blue blazer and khaki combination is one they'll wear over and over again. The ties were a thank you gift from the bride and groom.

NATURAL BEAUTY: IN AND OUT

It takes energy to plan a wedding. However, don't leave yourself drained for your trip down the aisle. Make natural beauty, inside and out, a priority in your planning. For a refreshing take on the old diet-and-exercise soapbox, consider our broader perspective on eco-beauty, compiled especially for organic gals (and guys, too).

We turned to Kat James, holistic beauty expert, health advocate, and founder of InformedBeauty.com <www.informedbeauty.com>, for her valuable advice and insight (read her interview on page 36-37). Kat is a recognized leader in reshaping our view of conventional beauty and body wisdom. Her motto is: "think health and beauty will follow." Through her website and her book, *The Truth about Beauty,* Kat offers the most up-to-date and well-rounded

"*I* told people for months ahead of my wedding that my dress was made from a hemp/silk blend fabric. Although most people refrained from making a wisecrack about smoking my dress after the wedding, I could see the skepticism in their faces because there is still so much confusion about what hemp is and what it is not. I was so excited to wear a beautiful gown made from an environmentally sustainable fabric and I am proud to be part of changing people's perspective on what hemp is, what it can look like and who wears it." — *Stacey*

HEMP 101

Is Hemp Really Just Marijuana?

No. A thousand times no. Hemp, also called industrial hemp, contains less than 1% THC (the psychoactive compound that produces the high in marijuana), as compared to 10% in marijuana. Hemp is cultivated for its long, extremely strong and durable fibers. This critical difference means if you smoke hemp, you get about the same effect as if you were to smoke cotton — a big headache and not much else.

Why do many people associate hemp with marijuana?

Unfortunately for industrial hemp, its leaves look nearly identical to its distant and illegal cousin, marijuana. Further confusing the issue for many is that the word "hemp" is considered a slang word for marijuana. Because of these suspicions and false impressions, cultivation of industrial hemp is illegal in the US, despite the fact that over 20 countries around the world actively cultivate it. Equating hemp and marijuana is like saying that eating poppy seeds on your morning bagel is the same as smoking opium. It's just not the case.

Why is industrial hemp an environmentally friendly fiber?

Hemp is one of the most versatile plants on earth. First, hemp is easily grown in most climates and is naturally pest-resistant, so it requires no pesticide use. Contrast that with cotton, which consumes 25 percent of the world's pesticides, despite making up only three percent of the world's crops. One acre of hemp yields three times more fiber than cotton. Hemp fiber is stronger than cotton fiber, which breaks down over time. Hemp is also naturally moisture resistant, which is why it was used for centuries to make rigging and sails for ships like the USS *Constitution*. Hemp is quickly grown and harvested in only four months — unlike trees, which take about 20 years to mature. One acre of hemp yields as much paper as four acres of trees. Hemp can be made into fuel, plastic, fabric, paper, cosmetics and food products, to name only a few. It can reduce our reliance on:

- Petroleum; a non-renewable fossil fuel that contributes to environmental degradation and political conflict around the world.
- Trees; our planet's lungs and a difficult resource to renew quickly.
- Cotton; a pesticide-intensive crop.

Why make wedding gowns from hemp/silk or hemp/Tencel® fabric?

Because it is beautiful, natural and earth-friendly. Hemp and silk are both renewable resources. Hemp fabric alone does not have the drape required for bridal wear. Hemp resembles linen or cotton. However, combining hemp with silk or Tencel® creates a gorgeous fabric well-suited to bridal gowns and other formal wear. For environmentally aware brides, a wedding gown that doesn't use synthetic petroleum-based fabric is a welcome and wonderful alternative.

EXERCISE YOUR OPTIONS

A regular program of exercise will not only keep you in shape, but is a great antidote to the stress that inevitably builds as your wedding day approaches. Whatever form of exercise you prefer, balance aerobic activities, which boost your heart rate, with a routine that stretches and tones your muscles. Yoga is one great way to stay limber and relaxed, and if you can't make it to a class, there are yoga videos you can follow at home. Exercise is a vital component to health, but remember that how we nourish ourselves and what we put on our skin are also critical.

information on natural and organic products to help you look and feel your best.

Countdown to the Big Day

By making smart upgrades, not by working harder, you can shed the mindset, toxins and excesses that hold back natural beauty. Don't just pile on every new product you find at the health food store without first discontinuing the things that can bury your beauty. Kat James offers these five steps for the seven to ten days (or longer) before your wedding: "Following these basic directions will go a long way to feeding your body and rebuilding yourself toward maximum radiance, on your wedding day and every day."

Step One: Say goodbye to sugar, caffeine and high-glycemic foods like white flour and white pasta. Sugar is natural beauty's number one enemy. If you want to see the shape of your face become more defined, your abdomen flatten out, your under-eye circles diminish, and your arms lose their puffiness, stop eating sugar and high-glycemic foods. Sugar and coffee can both aggravate skin problems. By cutting out sugar and caffeine, and upgrading to a caffeine-free beverage (such as Teeccino <www.teeccino.com>), you will discover an amazing way to reenergize yourself. Sugar makes insulin, which signals the body to store fat. Replace white carbohydrates with brown rice or barley. But moderation is everything; carbs should be kept in line with enough protein to balance the diet. The encouraging thing is, even if you start cutting out sugar just a couple of days before your wedding, it takes only two or three days to see and feel a huge difference.

Step Two: Drink organic green tea and lots of water every day. Organic green tea is a top-notch beauty beverage. It reduces inflammation, burns fat, makes your teeth healthy and is a skin antioxidant. It also has theanine, which is a natural anti-stress chemical. Green tea keeps you energized but de-stressed, with about 30 mg of caffeine per cup as compared to 110-175 mg in coffee. Switch

This bride is wearing
a hemp/Tencel® blend
strapless ball gown.
The bodice has an
overlay of embroidered
and beaded silk gauze
and there is an overskirt
of silk gauze. Her veil is
silk organza.

Natural Nuptials

SALLY AND GENE — SEPTEMBER 7
COASTAL MAINE

Sally and Gene's picturesque coastal Maine wedding took place only steps from the Atlantic Ocean, where breathtaking views formed a perfect backdrop for this sea-loving couple. Unaware they were nearly neighbors for most of their lives in both Pennsylvania and Delaware, the couple met in Maine. They enjoy sailing and have a deep appreciation for the ecology and natural beauty of Maine's seacoast.

In planning for their eco-friendly wedding, they started with eye-catching invitations made from handmade, recycled paper embedded with wildflower seeds. They used an eco-friendly vellum paper overlay tied with a fresh cedar sprig. The talented couple not only designed and printed their own invitations, but chose a 100% post-consumer waste recycled paper for their wedding programs.

Sally's custom gown was made using a hemp/silk blend fabric with a silk gauze overlay and train. Gene wore a coordinating hemp/silk vest and a locally found antique 18th century shirt, carefully restored then tailored by a seamstress. The bride found stylish rentals for the bridesmaids' gowns and the groomsmen's attire. For wedding rings, the couple designed their own with the help of an artist in southern Maine, who also hand-crafted them.

The couple's seaside reception, next to the ceremony site, took place outside ☞

Natural Nuptials

☞ under a tent. A harpist played beautiful music both throughout the ceremony and after, while the couple greeted their 150 guests. For the bride and groom, the sense of community was one of the most memorable elements. Many friends and family lent a hand in the preparations. "The most important aspect of our wedding was our vows to each other," said Sally. "We also wanted it to be a time for our families and friends to get to know each other. It was overwhelming to receive so much love and support, and to see these different parts of our lives intersect." All the food at the reception was organic and vegan, with most fresh ingredients sourced locally. Beverages included organic wines and locally brewed beer. Lavish arrays of organic flowers were selected from several neighbors' gardens and the couple's home. The flowers were taken to a local florist, who arranged them. For a special touch, a few of Gene's vibrant home-cultivated orchids graced Sally's upswept hair, as well as his own bouton-niere. The couple wanted non-electric lighting for the reception, so they used oil lamps encircled with greens and dried statice in purple and pink

hues as centerpieces. They rented linens, dishes and silverware, rather than use any disposables.

Their distinctive reception favors, smooth stones that the couple embellished with hand-written inspirational quotes from their favorite poets and authors, were placed at each seat. Hinting at the favors to be discovered, a sign out-side the tent instructed guests, "Please sit wher-ever you feel so inspired," which added a touch of delight and creativity to seating arrangements. The symbol of the tree is important to both Gene and Sally, so guests also received tree seed kits, further representing the couple's desire to live lightly on the Earth. As the setting sun col-ored the sky, the couple took a few moments for themselves and walked along the beach, as music from the local band carried on the sea breeze. Later on, while the evening began to wind down, the heavens treated the delighted group to a spectacular display of Northern Lights. With many special memories of their wedding to cherish, the couple left a few days later for a honeymoon sailing the Maine coast in their boat, which Gene had masterfully restored. 🍃

Our "five-step" inside-and-out natural beauty advice holds true for the guys, too. They also need a good night's sleep, healthy eating and exercise, as well as environmentally sound and chemical free personal care products.

your sugary beverages (including fruit juices) to green tea or water. Choose whole fruits instead of fruit juices, and try to drink about eight glasses of water every day, some of which can be decaffeinated teas. Besides being great for your health, water is a natural appetite suppressant.

Step Three: Feed your natural beauty with fiber and essential fatty acids. Stress and jitters create excess hormones and toxins, which can be processed by the liver but stay in the body. The best way to remove them is through good sources of fiber. De-tox with a diet high in flax, berries, brown rice and greens. Essential fatty acids like supplements, flax, fish oil or evening primrose oil will help nourish your skin in a relatively short period of time. The same goes for your hair, but you'll need three months to see a real change there.

Step Four: Eliminate artificial ingredients and harsh exfoliants from your skin-care regimen. If you have any skin challenges, Kat suggests a review of the ingredients in every skin care product you use and elimination of perfumes, petrochemicals, detergents, added fragrances, artificial colors and as many preservatives as possible. These ingredients wage a synthetic assault on your body. Stop using foaming cleansers and facial soaps containing sodium lauryl sulfate. Switch to cleansing milks, which are gentler and don't strip away natural oils. If you have oily skin, the tendency is to want to dry out the oils by scrubbing with soap. However, this tactic can cause a rebound, signaling your skin to produce more oil. Be sure to try out any new products at least two weeks before the wedding to avoid any skin surprises close to your big day.

Step Five: Get your beauty sleep. Adequate sleep is critical. During sleep, there is circulation to your face, and deep sleep prompts the human growth hormone to do its beauty magic throughout your body. If the wedding excitement is making it hard to get to sleep, be sure not to have caffeine or other stimulating foods within six hours of bedtime. Don't exercise strenuously before going to sleep, but instead try some relaxation techniques or slow yoga stretches and deep breathing. Try pampering yourself with a soothing aromatherapy bath of pure essential oils.

Kiss and Makeup

For your wedding day look, Kat advises, "First and foremost, be yourself. If you don't wear makeup or wear very little, then the worst thing you can do is have someone overload you on your wedding day." Here are some ways to let your natural look shine through.

Get ready for that first kiss by avoiding the plethora of petroleum-based lip products on the market. They only make things worse by actually reducing your lip moisture level — which is why after using them for a while you feel like you can't live without them. After much field testing of non-petroleum lip balms, high on our list for natural lip protection are: Dr. Hauschka's Lip Care Stick, John Masters' Lip Calm and Terressentials Lip Balm. However, if your lips are already roughed up, don't lick and chew them. Give them a chance to heal before your trip down the aisle. Avoid using matte lipsticks, which are very drying. Opt instead for a thin, sheer gloss like Lavera's Lip Gloss. For more definition and a touch of color, outline your lips with a lip pencil. Kat advises, "Makeup should never be a mask — the point is to soften anything that distracts from your best features. Then, slightly augment your best features with neutral tones."

If you hire a hair or makeup professional, be sure he or she understands your taste and style. "Many professionals feel compelled to spend at least 30 or 40 minutes doing something that should take 10," says Kat. The up-do is not a must-do. Take into account your hair's natural personality. Depending on your personal style and desired look, a trusted friend or family member might be better suited to help you with a simple hairstyle and applying a little makeup. Test it out ahead of time to be sure of the results.

MAKEUP MAGIC

We asked Kat to share her top choices for natural cosmetics:

- Concealer? "Anne Marie Borlind has a nice slightly gold one."
- Powder/Foundation? "Always look for golden tones regardless of how light or dark your skin. Rose and pink tones can be disastrous."
- Blush? "Dr. Hauschka's golden peach tone blushes are flattering on nearly all skin tones."
- Mascara? "Anne Marie Borlind's mascara has great colors. Top lashes only!"
- Lip Pencil? "Jane Iredale's or Lavera — both are great."
- Lip Gloss? "Jane Iredale's melon and raspberry colors are favorites for all skin tones."
- Eye Shadow? "Jane Iredale completely wins for pure eye shadow selection."
- Hair spray? "Aubrey Organics, but don't go wild — use only what you need to secure the style."

Words of Wisdom

*K*at James experienced first-hand the power of a profound personal transformation. On the brink of a health crisis, Kat became an information junkie and is now on the forefront of creating a new awareness of how nutrition and beauty choices not only impact personal health, but also the future health of the planet. Through her website <www.informedbeauty.com>; her book, *The Truth about Beauty*; and her Total Transformation™ cruises, Kat is redefining real beauty and its deep connections to our inner health and the natural world around us.

Organic Weddings: Who or what shaped your life with respect to the values we see in your company and career?

Kat James: It took an eating disorder, a personal health crisis, and my denatured lifestyle for me to realize that I was a disconnected person, not in touch with the power of nature and the importance of true sustenance. Doctors were telling me my only choice was to live on an awful drug that lowers immunity, causes depression and half the time doesn't even work. That was my turning point. I shifted my motivation from beauty and weight to health. I wandered into a health food store, picked up my first non-diet health book, and, after reversing my illness, went from being an herbal atheist to a believer. Making that change is also what opened my eyes to the issue of sustainability. I learned about the chemistry of my food cravings and turned that around. I cured a number of my own minor and major health and beauty problems, like skin problems, just by changing what I put on and in my body. Since then, I've made a career out of finding well-researched information and sharing it.

OW: What element of your work do you most enjoy?

KJ: I enjoy showing people ways to marry their desire for treating themselves better and feeling more beautiful with the appeal of doing something good for the planet. By quantifying beauty benefits as simple lifestyle upgrades, I skip the monotony of typical health advice, or the ☞

Words of Wisdom (contd.)

☞ obligation to become an activist in order to make a difference. After people have adjusted their routines and I tell them they're also sparing the planet by not sending more synthetic toxins down the drain and into our water supply, they're thrilled and begin to see the bigger picture – the connection between taking care of their health and the health of the planet.

OW: How can brides continue to express their own style and values when determining their wedding look?

KJ: Whether we're talking about beauty or values, brides can be misled into thinking that this special occasion means that being true to oneself and one's personal values are suspended for a day. Too often, they put choices that should be very personal into the hands of conventional professionals. An example of this is the conventional wedding planner who whips up an affair that has nothing to do with the couple's deeper values. It's much more meaningful to begin that first day of your lives together reflecting the values to which you aspire. Shouldn't your "dream day" be the ultimate in expressing what you hope for your lives and the world?

OW: What is something you do in your own home to reduce your ecological footprint?

KJ: I eat a lot of organic food, and I give up an extra lipstick or a pair of shoes every year to do it. I use a shower purifier with a high-pressure spray. It reduces the amount of water I use, while saving my skin and hair a lot of abuse. Also, I don't use personal care products that send more environmental toxins down the drain. An EPA study has shown that all the waterways in the US are contaminated with every personal care product and drug you can think of, as well as the drugs used in raising livestock. Because pesticides and chemicals are particularly prevalent in animal products, I make it a rule to eat only organic eggs, butter, yogurt and other dairy products. Everything that you buy and eat can reduce your burden on the environment.

OW: Why organic weddings?

KJ: We can let our beauty ripple outward. Whether that applies to the choices you make regarding your own beauty, or your concern about making an impact on our future – either way it's a win-win situation. Your wedding day leaves a legacy in your life, in your conscience, and in your authenticity; it's one of those meaningful experiences you can share with your partner that is elevated and beyond appearances. 🐚

ECO-BEAUTY LEADERS

These companies are recognized leaders in the 4 Ps of Eco-beauty: purity, practices, packaging and performance:

- Aubrey Organics
- Colorganics
- Dr. Hauschka
- Erbaviva
- John Masters
- Jules and Jane
- Lavera
- Terressentials
- Trillium Herbal
- Weleda

The Four Ps of Eco-beauty: Purity, Practices, Packaging and Performance

With many beauty products competing for recognition as natural, organic or eco-friendly, our best advice is to determine your own priorities. Regarding her own beauty regimen, Kat says, "I've minimized perfume, most petrochemicals and artificial colors. Everyone should assess their beauty products and decide which ones best balance ecological considerations and individual appeal."

Purity and Performance. "Purity is the new decadence," Kat says. "If it never goes bad, it can't make you beautiful." A chemical soup of preservatives, synthetic colors, petrochemicals, detergents and fragrance makes up those long lists of ingredients you can barely pronounce on beauty product labels. Debates rage on whether preservatives like methylparaben, one of those used the longest in cosmetics and toiletries, is more or less likely to cause a reaction than natural preservatives such as citrus seed extract. In reality, reactions are possible with either. However, Kat points out that some of the products using synthetic preservatives are the painstakingly harvested biodynamic products, which may most actively deliver beauty benefits to you.

Practices and Packaging. Most companies that are serious about what they put into their bottles tend toward environmentally and socially responsible business practices, as well as minimal, eco-friendly packaging. Some beauty product companies tout green manufacturing innovations. Others highlight their use of natural and organic plant-based ingredients. However, many of these same companies also use synthetic colors, fragrance, or preservatives such as parabens and the formaldehyde-releasing diazolidinyl urea. In these cases, it is up to each individual to decide how to weigh the elements of purity, performance, practices and packaging.

GEMS AND JEWELS

As a conscientious consumer, buying wedding jewelry can be one of the situations where mainstream practices conflict with your values. In addition to the negative environmental impact of mining precious metals and gemstones, diamonds — ultra-popular for engagement and wedding jewelry — are associated with environmental degradation, political turmoil, human rights violations and market manipulation. Diamonds, while beautiful, are not so much rare treasures of nature, as they are squirreled away by a savvy industry that manages supply and demand to keep prices high and consumer desire peaked. Around 1940, DeBeers, the largest diamond mining and distribution company in the world, launched their now famous and still ongoing "A Diamond is Forever" advertising campaign, fueling widespread desire to own a diamond engagement ring.

SCENTS AND SENSIBILITY

"Fragrance is a big irritant," Kat warns. "Conventional perfumes can ruin your day." She reminds us that the chemicals found in perfumes don't have to be listed. "You've got up to 200 or more chemicals, usually including known pollutants and neurotoxins, in conventional perfumes," says Kat. For those who can't imagine their wedding ensemble without a little dab of something lovely-smelling, try a blend of essential oils from natural fragrance expert Mandy Aftel. Mandy's company, Aftelier <www.aftelier.com>, in Berkeley, California, specializes in using only natural oils to create fragrance. Mandy offers both ready-to-wear and custom blends, both of which are perfect for a bride. "For weddings, I like to use pure essences from flowers like jasmine, Moroccan rose, boronia, and magnolia; from fruits like blood orange and pink grapefruit; or from desserts, like vanilla or chocolate," Mandy says. "I've created new scents for many brides, as well as bridesmaids, or even something for a bride and groom." Natural cosmetics company Jules and Jane also offers a unique blend of essential oils called *Eau* that can be worn by bride or groom.

The Fifth C: Conflict.

The industry standard for valuing all diamonds are the Four Cs: cut, color, clarity and carat weight. In recent years, a fifth C has emerged: Conflict. An estimated 3-5% of all the diamonds that make it to the retail marketplace today are suspected of originating in certain areas in Africa where rough (uncut) diamonds are sold to finance wars, resulting in human rights violations. There is even strong evidence that global terrorist organizations profit from trade in conflict diamonds.

"*I* decided against packing my gown away in the attic. Instead, I chose to save my wedding dress to pass on by selling it and putting the money into a Certificate of Deposit (CD). By the time my own daughter (or my son's bride-to-be) walks down the aisle, the account balance will more than provide a dream gown for her."

— *Maria*

In January 2003, to stop the flow of 'conflict diamonds,' the diamond industry initiated a requirement that all rough diamonds be first sold (to diamond cutters, for example) with a certificate of origin. Unfortunately, these certificates are not passed along to the retailer, so it's important to work with a jeweler you trust who is confident of the stone's origin. Alternately, buy an estate piece that predates these war conflicts or buy diamonds mined in Canada, where environmental regulations are very strict. Diamonds that predate the 1880s even avoid the environmental issues associated with the onset of large scale, destructive mining techniques. According to the Gemological Institute of America, about 250 tons of earth has to be mined to produce a single 1-carat diamond.

A decidedly modern way to keep the tradition of a wedding diamond but avoid its unfortunate environmental or social impacts is to look into the economical alternative of a man-made or "cultured" diamond from Gemesis <www.gemesis.com> or Apollo Diamond <www.apollodiamond.com>. These companies are leading a revolution to create low impact gems, which technically are real diamonds, and are virtually indistinguishable from mined diamonds. Even diamond experts admit that one of the only hints to their origin is that they are flawless, which is extremely rare in natural diamonds. These diamonds are created in machines that combine tiny elements of carbon with extreme pressure and heat to mimic the process that occurs within the Earth to produce a diamond.

To address the negative issues of mechanized mining of precious metals like gold, GreenKarat <www.greenkarat.com> offers couples environmentally responsible wedding jewelry. GreenKarat sells rings and other items made from responsibly mined gold, called Certified Green Gold™, as well as items made using recycled metals. "The Certified Green Gold™ program helps preserve biodiversity in the mined areas, while also offering sustainable solutions to the social and economic needs of the local communities," said Matthew White, founder of GreenKarat.

Something Old, Something New

Options for wedding jewelry include family sources, buying new, buying old (also called "estate"), or custom made. With a new ring, the best option is to choose the stone and mounting separately. Buying a loose stone allows you to see any flaws that reduce a stone's value, as mountings can hide these. Estate jewelry is pre-owned — think recycled — and categorized as contemporary, vintage (within the last 100 years), or antique (100 years or older). An estate ring is almost always purchased intact with the stones mounted and generally at a lower price than you would pay for a new piece. You can keep the piece as-is in appreciation of the craftsmanship or historical significance, or have the stones remounted into a new setting. Custom-made jewelry is a nice option because in many situations, you work directly with a local artisan or designer to create a unique piece, plus support your local small business economy. This option is also a meaningful way to recycle any old or under-used fine jewelry you may have. Gold, in particular, is easily melted down (called smelting) and remade into something new.

These flower girls are wearing hemp/silk dresses with silk eyelet overskirts.

Other wedding day jewelry — necklaces, bracelets, cufflinks, and more — make memorable and practical gifts for wedding party attendants, or for the bride and groom to exchange with each other (see page 101 for more gift suggestions). It is also a perfect opportunity to borrow a piece of family jewelry to wear for added sentimentality. Thinking of splurging on a tiara? Services are available to recycle it after the big day into a more useful piece of jewelry, such as a necklace or bracelet, by restringing the gems or pearls. Above all, whatever you choose for your wedding jewelry, the most important aspect is that it is in step with your values, right for you as a couple and embodies the love that you share for each other.

ECO-CHIC ON THE GO

Packing for your honeymoon yet? Fashionable selections of eco-friendly clothing for men and women are plentiful. If you find you're lacking that perfect little black (organic cotton) dress, or maybe something more casual, use the links below to find beautiful items that will last for years in both durability and style. These companies are dedicated to bringing you clothes made using planet and people friendly ideas: earth-friendly fabrics, low-impact dyes and fair trade practices. For the eco-savvy, sustainability is always in vogue.

- coolnotcruel <www.coolnotcruel.com>
- Indigenous Designs <www.indigenousdesigns.com>
- Patagonia <www.patagonia.com>
- Rawganique <www.rawganique.com>
- Under the Canopy <www.underthecanopy.com>
- Wildlife Works <www.wildlife-works.com>

CHAPTER 4

Tree-free and Recycled Invitations

B EFORE ANYONE SEES YOUR WEDDING ATTIRE or tastes that delicious organic food at your reception, the invitation will set the tone for your celebration. Your wedding stationery is a perfect opportunity to be eco-friendly right from the start. Be sure that your wedding invitations and other correspondence are printed on tree-free and recycled paper. There are many eye-catching earth-friendly choices. You won't be sacrificing style and will be making a difference in an area of critical ecological importance. Whether casual, traditional or ultra-formal, wedding invitations vary considerably, but once you choose your perfect words, they deserve nothing less than to be printed on the best: tree-free and recycled paper.

REASONS FOR RECYCLED

Why bother with recycled paper? According to the Recycled Paper Coalition <www.papercoalition.org>, more than 90% of the printing and writing paper

> "
> A nation that destroys its soil destroys itself. Forests are the lungs of our land, purifying the air and giving fresh strength to our people.
> — Franklin Delano Roosevelt
> "

made in the US today is *still virgin paper.* The EPA reports that paper in its various forms accounts for 40% of all solid waste generated. Office paper comprises a quarter of that, with less than 20% recovered for recycling.

Papermaking is a messy business, requiring huge amounts of water and energy. The chemicals used to bleach the paper result in toxic by-products, notably dioxin. Above all, producing new paper eats up trees, putting intense pressure on forest resources in this country and worldwide. This growing shortage of wood fiber encourages the environmentally catastrophic practice of clearcutting, in which a forest is simply razed until no tree is left standing. Many trees are cut from our ever-shrinking ancient forests, which support complex ecosystems. When this happens, all wildlife goes and the once-fertile

Future Forests
ONE SEEDLING AT A TIME

Where trees have been clearcut, especially in rocky soil or on steep terrain, the forest needs a hand in order to come back to life. Looking at the wasteland left by a clearcut, it can be hard to imagine that the forest will ever regenerate. However, there are crews of tenacious treeplanters whose job is to do just that: one by one, they dig holes and set new seedlings in the ground. It's incredibly strenuous physical labor. Treeplanters haul 30-pound bags of seedlings back and forth for miles each day, shovel each hole, and bend to drop in a seedling about 200 times per hour. All this must be done in full exposure to heat, rain, freezing cold, blackflies, and other elements. Besides the physical grind, it's also hard for planters to avoid exposure to the array of pesticides sprayed on seedlings while at the nursery. One treeplanter can seed around 1,300 trees in a day, and in Canada 650 million seedlings are planted each year.

topsoil is left to erode away. Each year the world loses 42 million acres of forest — an area about the size of New England. More than three-quarters of the world's old-growth forests have already been logged or degraded, much of this within the past three decades. ReThink Paper <www.rethinkpaper.org> reports that less than five percent of our original forests remain in the United States.

Recycling can provide some relief. Recycling paper, rather than using virgin fiber, saves trees, energy, and water, and requires less bleaching and fewer noxious chemicals. The recycling process also concentrates inks, chemicals, and other hazardous waste, which can then be disposed of responsibly instead of being scattered throughout landfills or into the atmosphere through incineration. The

Often the crews — students, immigrants, travelers, and seasonal workers — find themselves far from any road, hiking with boxes of seedlings to barren patches of clearcut land. Or they may reach a remote wilderness planting site by helicopter, boat, or all-terrain vehicle. The practice of replanting logging sites used to be rare; nature was expected to take over and raise a new forest. However, beginning in the 1970s, in response to the scale of industrial logging, large tree planting efforts became a common part of forestry. Now, many state and provincial governments require logging companies to pay for reforestation efforts. Even under these regulations, it takes many years for a clearcut forest to return to a healthy ecosystem, capable of providing wildlife habitat and maintaining soil and water balances. Many retired treeplanters go on to work as advocates for reducing clearcutting and finding more sustainable ways to harvest a forest.
(Photo and information from *Handmade Forests: The Treeplanter's Experience*, by Hélène Cyr).

CHLORINE AND DIOXINS

Chlorine is used in papermaking to turn wood chips into paper pulp, as well as to bleach the paper to a bright white. Besides the health hazard of direct exposure to chlorine, making paper with this chemical creates byproducts known as dioxins and organochlorines, both highly toxic chemicals. Dioxins are released into the environment through the wastes from paper mills, and from there they make it into our air, soil, and the food chain. Research has linked these chemicals to cancer, birth defects, and reproductive disorders, making them some of the most critical substances to stop dumping in our environment. In fact, an EPA study found dioxins to be 300,000 times more potent as a carcinogen than the banned pesticide DDT. More benign chemicals, such as hydrogen peroxide, are just as capable of bleaching paper — so look for "non-chlorine bleached" items whenever possible.

fibers in a sheet of paper can be recycled up to a dozen times before they become too short for new paper.

You can do your part by recycling paper and cardboard whenever possible, and by cutting down your paper use. Think twice before you hit the "print" button and print double-sided when you do. Also, be sure you buy recycled paper with *post consumer* content (paper from people's recycling bins). You might think all recycled papers are created equal, but labeling guidelines set by the Federal Trade Commission only require that recycled paper be made from so-called "recovered" materials. What's misleading about this category is that recovered paper may just mean that scraps and trimmings from virgin papermaking were tossed back into the pulp vats — a practice that papermakers have always followed simply because it makes economic sense. However, for recycling to really work, community collection programs need to be tied into strong recycled paper markets to survive. To close the loop, the paper you toss in a recycling bin has to be re-made into new paper. That's why it's important to look closely and choose products and paper with the highest post-consumer content you can find. This book is printed on 30 percent post-consumer waste (PCW) recycled paper — among the highest PCW content for a coated paper. Be vocal about wanting to see *at least* 30 percent post-consumer waste recycled paper in your office supply store, but 100 percent is best.

TREE-FREE IS TERRIFIC

Alternatives to paper made from trees are not as radical as you might think. For hundreds, even thousands of years, paper was made of everything *but* trees — from textile scraps to cotton, flax, and hemp. It wasn't until the 1860s

that paper-making from trees was intro-
duced. Today, there is a growing supply of
high-quality options for papers that are
totally tree-free:

Kenaf: This is a fibrous plant related
to cotton and okra, which looks like a
beanstalk and grows up to 15 feet in five
months. One acre of kenaf yields around
three to five times as many pounds of fiber as a same-sized plot of Southern pine,
a favorite for papermaking. As it is harvested for its fiber rather than its flowers,
no insecticides are necessary.

Industrial Hemp: Although it contains insignificant amounts of any drug,
hemp growing in the US was essentially banned in the 1930s. Before that,

however, it was relied on for centuries as a sturdy fiber used in everything from rope to the first pair of Levi's jeans. Learn more about hemp on page 29.

Textile scraps: Cotton, denim and linen scraps make great paper because of their durable fibers, and this also saves valuable material from getting tossed into a landfill.

Recycled money: Take a close look at a dollar bill; what you'll see is tiny fibers because US currency is made from cotton and linen, rather than trees. With the amount of times a bill changes hands before it's retired, it has to be durable. It also recycles well.

In many cases, these tree-free fibers are blended with post-consumer waste recycled paper and are also chlorine-free. Together these elements create the ideal eco-friendly paper. Why? Tree-free fibers help take the burden off trees, which are too valuable to use for creating throw-away products like paper. Blended papers go even further by closing the recycling loop, creating demand for post consumer waste products and supporting manufacturers that don't use chlorine bleach.

PIECE IT TOGETHER

Just how many printed pieces will you need for your wedding celebration? While not all of these are necessary, here are the traditional items. They add up, so put it all on tree-free and recycled paper, and be sure to include a description of these special papers somewhere to share the knowledge and inspire others to follow your lead.

• Engagement announcements
• Save-the-date cards
• Engagement/shower gift thank-you notes
• Wedding invitations
• Reply cards and reception cards

"My husband and I love trees and focused on their importance in our life as a theme throughout our wedding plans. We used all recycled and tree-free papers for our invitation. We gave "Tree in a Box" favors and included readings and music in our ceremony that were symbolic of our connection with nature and how that connection brought us together. Planning a ceremony that was unique to us was more work than just taking something straight from a book, but it turned out beautifully. I think the most important thing a marrying couple can do is to follow their own hearts. They must determine what or who means the most to them as they celebrate joining together. Those other voices that tell you what or what not to do vanish as quickly as they appear, but you will carry those first moments of your marriage with your forever."

— Sara

LEARN TO BE FOREST-FRIENDLY

From your mailbox to your living room, at work and online, there are many ways to reduce the wood resources that you consume. The average American uses 730 pounds of paper every year. Co-Op America has produced the WoodWise Guide <www.wood-wise.org> to help you cut back on the wood products you consume. Here are a few suggestions:

- **Reduce junk mail:**
  File a written request with the Direct Mail Association, which will get you off many mass-mailing lists. Avoid contests, which are often used to compile mailing lists, and sign up for e-statements and automatic payments for some or all of your monthly bills.

- **Buy certified wood:**
  Look for the checkmark of the Forest Stewardship Council when buying lumber or furniture. Certification means the product complies with international standards for responsible forestry.

- **Urge magazines to print on recycled paper:**
  Magazines alone eat up 35 million trees a year. That doesn't even take into account all the newspapers, catalogues, and phone books found in every home. You can use the pre-paid subscription cards that come in every magazine to give the publishers your suggestions for going green.

- Ceremony programs
- Menu cards
- Reception place cards
- Wedding announcements
- Wedding gift thank-you notes
- Name change/change of address cards

Try to avoid making or purchasing invitations that have non-recyclable elements, such as plastic or other heavily coated papers. They are not only petroleum-based, but are not accepted as recyclable plastic. Skipping excess frills and ultra-formalities will cut down on the waste your invitations generate. Many couples are choosing to minimize their paper impact with these great ideas:

- Design your invitation to efficiently use paper.
- Use a reply postcard instead of a card and envelope.
- Don't use an inner envelope — a tradition carried over from the Pony Express days when outer envelopes were likely to get ruined in the post.
- Forget the tissue paper — another holdover from the time when tissue was enclosed to absorb slow-drying ink.
- Forgo a separate reception card — it is only needed if some of your guests will be invited to the ceremony, but not to the reception. Otherwise, the name and location of the reception can go on the invitation.

- Use double-sided printing whenever possible to minimize paper quantity. One example is to put a map on the back of your invitation.
- Use quantity-appropriate printing methods and vegetable-based inks whenever possible because they release fewer VOCs (volatile organic compounds) than petroleum-based inks. VOCs contribute to air pollution and can create health problems in workers.

Having trouble finding just the right words for your occasion? Visit the website Verse It <www.verseit.com> for wording suggestions.

THINK ABOUT THE INK

We're often asked what type of printing method is best for the environment. However, there is no single right answer. The main culprits are the ink or toner, the solvents needed to clean ink presses, and the electricity required to run the machines. In total, printing is not a very environmentally friendly thing to do. However, wedding tradition calls for the power of the printed word, so the best you can do is to minimize your impact by choosing a printing method that is right for your quantity, style and budget:

Handwritten or hand stamped invitations. This is a traditional and beautiful way to invite a smaller group to your nuptials. It's also quite eco-excellent as it uses no electricity and minimal ink. If you have a calligrapher or artist in the family, this option might work even for a larger number of invitations.

Digital or desktop printing. For do-it-yourselfers, quick turnaround requirements, or for invitations with many layers, digital

Invitations made from tree-free and recycled fibers, like this one of hemp and post-consumer waste content are elegant *and* eco-friendly.

Natural Nuptials

KIM AND KALANI — NOVEMBER 9
SAN JOSE, CALIFORNIA

Kalani surprised Kim with a memorable proposal on a beach in Belize, after managing to hide the engagement ring for the first eight days of their vacation. "I wanted to wait for the right time, even though it was tricky making sure she didn't see it," said Kalani. After returning from their tropical vacation, the couple set

about planning their eco-friendly wedding. "We both wanted it to be simple, but elegant, and to incorporate environmentally friendly ideas," said Kim.

Kim's strong environmental values motivated her to find ways to make their wedding green, even when it took perseverance and research to find the best solution. They minimized their paper use by printing their map and hotel information on the back of their panel-style invitation. They chose a response postcard, rather than a separate card and envelope, which saved paper again. A note on the bottom of the invitation let their guests know the paper was tree-free, and asked them to recycle it. "If there's something ecological about your wedding, I think it's important to let your guests know," said Kim. "Earth friendly things are not always obvious, but spreading the word helps people see that it can be done tastefully."

For their venue, they chose the San Jose Museum of Art in order to support public arts awareness, and especially because the non-profit museum relies on special events and donations for income rather than charging admission fees. "It was important ☞

Natural Nuptials

☞ to us that our money would support the arts, whereas we felt if the reception had been at a hotel, our money would go to putting in new carpets or something," said Kim. The museum accommodated both the ceremony and reception, and was located next door to a hotel and a light rail station. The streamlined logistics were both eco-savvy and appreciated by their guests, who didn't have to face any transportation headaches.

Already set amongst priceless works of art, their event didn't need any additional decorations. The only flowers at the wedding were in Kim's small bouquet and in Kalani's boutonniere. Yet, it was their avant-garde "flower girl" who stole the show. Kalani's 22-year-old brother Scott walked down the aisle scattering tiny maple-leaf-shaped cutouts from the couple's junk mail, made using decorative hole punchers from a craft store. "You should have seen the looks on our guests' faces when they saw what landed on the ground," said Kim. The handmade touch accented other details of their reception, from individually stamped, homemade paper place cards to the stunning sculptural centerpiece bowls hand-crafted by Kalani's uncle, a professional woodworker. Not only did the bowls look beautiful on the tables, but they also held a variety of fresh breads provided by the couple's caterer. Another charming aspect to the reception was Kim and Kalani's personalized take on table markers — instead of numbers, they assigned each table a name in honor of a place they'd hiked or backpacked together, like the Grand Canyon. Each table got a photo of the couple standing in front of a sign that marked the destination, and guests had a great time venturing from table to table, looking at all the snapshots.

While they chose a DJ to get the crowd dancing during the reception, Kim and Kalani hired members of the California Youth Symphony to provide music during the ceremony and cocktail hour. The string quintet needed no electricity and the young musicians, aged 14-17, played expertly for a reasonable fee. Kim and Kalani's commitment to reducing their wedding's environmental impact led them to plan a beautiful event filled with many meaningful touches. 🎎

WOW — WHY ORGANIC WEDDINGS?

Every year US farms produce 250 million tons of agricultural residues, fibrous leftovers such as stalks and leaves from harvested crops. To get rid of this waste product, the residues are usually burned, polluting the air with particulates and emissions, and posing a health and safety risk for farm communities. Work is underway to convert agricultural residues into much-needed fiber for paper, building materials, textiles, and more. With the industry shortage of wood fiber, this alternative source of fiber can be an environmentally sound and economically viable solution for farms. (Source: Fiber Futures <www.fiberfutures.org>)

printing or desktop printing with a laser or inkjet printer is a likely candidate. Even though toner from laser and digital printers is petroleum based (don't forget to recycle your cartridges), these types of printing have definite environmental benefits: no industrial waste is created as with liquid ink printing, no cleaning solvents are required after each job, and no printing plates are made for each original, since printing is done directly from computer to paper. A new type of digital printing uses solid ink cartridges. Like big Crayons®, these wax blocks melt, requiring no cartridge disposal or recycling.

Offset, Thermography, Letterpress or Engraved Printing. With these options, exact methods vary, but basically plates are made for each original, and then printed using ink on a printing press. These printing options are more expensive, but also provide higher end finishes. If you choose any of these methods for your invitations, ask your printer to use non-petroleum based inks, such as soy or vegetable inks, which are made from renewable resources. Soy-based inks emit fewer VOCs than petroleum inks, contributing less air pollution, and they are also easier to de-ink in the recycling process. You might also ask if the print shop uses less toxic solvents to clean their presses, which can be a health concern for workers, as well being as an environmental issue. Handling of leftover used ink is another concern because it is an industrial waste that requires proper disposal.

CHAPTER 5

A Ceremony to Cherish

L ET YOUR CEREMONY BE THE FOCAL POINT of your marriage celebration and allow it to illustrate both your connection with each other and to environmental and social causes. Don't leave ceremony decisions to the very end. Making the time to research and craft a memorable, meaningful event can put other planning details in perspective. Take a deep breath and remember the purpose of the wedding is to *wed* you and your loved one together, which is an invisible yet momentous step in your lives.

There can be a lot of pressure to make everything perfect, or keep everyone happy, or for this to be the best day of your life. No matter your situation, there is no correct or ideal wedding, only the one that is right for you. Let the transformation that you're going through, individually and as a couple, remain the heart and soul of the wedding.

Treat the Earth well.
It was not given to
you by your parents.
It was loaned to you
by your children.
— Kenyan proverb

When you are making choices for your ceremony, keep in mind how you can combine location, ritual, décor, vows and more to craft a magical event celebrating your appreciation of love, community and nature. We've gathered recommendations and tips to help you plan. Don't be shy; ask your loved ones to participate. Involve them in your ceremony by asking them to read poems or passages, or play music. The presence and support of family and friends at your ceremony is a special part of your wedding day that you will remember for years to come.

THE PURPOSE OF RITUAL

> *The wedding ritual and the promises you make within it can become the trellis on which you will plant the vine of your relationship, something to support you and your relationship throughout your life together.*
> — Ann Keeler Evans, *Promises to Keep*

Unique, heartfelt vows, readings and rituals give you an opportunity to personalize your wedding. You'll bring tears of joy and smiles of approval to the faces of friends and family. It is also an opportunity to share your enthusiasm for the world around you by including passages that focus on the timeless beauty of nature. You can choose to write your entire ceremony or, if you are having a traditional religious ceremony, augment it with sections that resonate with your ideals and personal beliefs.

The mainstream wedding industry has sugar-coated marriage into an almost unrecognizable confection of bubbles and baubles. Many brides will devote more time and consideration to their wedding ensemble than to the design of their nuptial ceremony and vows. Plainly said, not enough attention is paid to the significant spiritual and personal changes both bride and groom experience.

To bring some perspective and priority back into the ritual of marriage, we turned to Ann Keeler Evans, a minister and author of *Promises to Keep: Crafting Your Wedding Ceremony*. Ann specializes in helping couples create ceremonies that reflect their beliefs and values. "You don't want a factory process that leaves you bent, folded, and stamped as "married" at the end, but rather something you create together as a gift that you then offer to your community. These steps lead you from unmarried to married," says Ann. "I think it's really important to avoid creating a ceremony you don't believe in. There are ways to make space for different family traditions and beliefs without feeling you've been run over by those

you want to please. A good officiant will help a marrying couple craft a ceremony that unifies the couple, as well as celebrates any differences in religious beliefs or culture."

CEREMONY ESSENTIALS

No matter if your ceremony is long or short, religious or secular, here's a five-part course of action to consider when planning your wedding ceremony. These elements, based on Ann's book, *Promises to Keep*, will help guide your thoughts on cherishing the magical moments as you become a married couple.

Part One: Welcome your guests to the ceremony. Invite the blessings of your guests according to your spiritual or religious beliefs. Establish a special connection with the place where you are marrying.

Begin your ceremony by recognizing that the people you love are at your ceremony to be with you and support you. Ann suggests, "Our communities are so virtual now. But this is our chance to put the stories together with the faces. It's not only important today, it's important for the future because these are the people who will gather around you in good times and hard times, through the years." A transformation is about to occur; two single people will be joined together into a married union. Set apart your ceremony site as a special place. Ann suggests, "If your wedding site is not used regularly for worship, declare it a special site because of the ritual taking place. If you are being married outside, give thanks for the beauty of nature."

Part Two: Recognize a marriage is a joining of two families. There are new relationships to be gained, however loosely or closely the families

PRACTICE MAKES PERFECT

Some may see the rehearsal as an unnecessary event. However, the upside to the rehearsal is that it clarifies the logistics, allowing you to concentrate more fully during your wedding ceremony on the special moments at hand. For vows, don't recite them if you want them to be a surprise, but still familiarize yourself with the flow of the ceremony. Choose attendants who will create serenity and connect you to your true nature. Remember, though, the wedding does *not* determine the success or failure of your relationship. So even if your day doesn't go as you imagined, let it be wonderful anyway. Relax and enjoy the presence of your loved ones, as well as your newlywed status.

bond together. Tell your guests why you are marrying and why this wonderful relationship will endure.

Take time to thank your families for all they have given you. Ask your families to welcome your partner and celebrate the future with you. Each person is becoming a member of the other's family. Ann adds, "Couples today are adults choosing to join their lives together. It's a chance to say what makes this relationship so important, and why you are committing to a lifetime of loving each other."

Part Three: Ask your guests to support your marriage. Provide a pledge of commitment for them to speak aloud. Include songs, readings or statements from friends and family to signify their support.

Your friends and families are there to help you celebrate, but also to hear you declare your love for each other out loud. Their investment in your relationship, nurturing and support are powerful things. Ann adds, "While it's not mandatory to include guest participation in readings or music for the ritual to be meaningful and complete, this element can really add inspiration to the event."

Part Four: State your vows — your promises — to each other and affirm your choice to marry one another. Exchange rings (or another token) as a symbol of your commitment.

WORDS TO LIVE BY

Getting started can sometimes be hard when you can't seem to find the right words. Sources for special quotations, verses and blessings are varied and countless. Common ones are Bible verses or other religious writings, books, poems and song lyrics. Some online sites, like Occasional Words <www.occasionalwords.com> offer writing services for poems and songs for special events like weddings. For more ideas and prayers to include in your ceremony, visit Ann Keeler Evans' web sites: A Rite to Remember <www.aritetoremember.com> and River Prayers <www.riverprayers.org>.

"*In* our wedding ceremony program, we took the time to write a few sentences about each member of our wedding party, to introduce them to our 325 guests. We explained how and when we met them and why they were so important in our lives. Everyone loved reading the stories and felt so much closer to our big wedding party of eight bridesmaids and eight groomsmen."

— *Kathy*

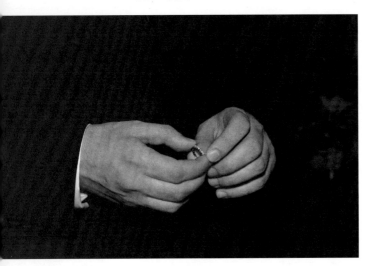

During your vows, you are saying to each other, "I love you and I'm going to be here." Formal language helps convey and honor the weight of your declaration. Find the appropriate words to celebrate this cherished covenant between partners. Ann suggests, "Vows are about saying what's already true, and finding words that make sense rather than just using somebody's rote vows. They need to say: 'I'm going to be the best person I can be; I'm going to support you as you continue to dream and grow; and this relationship will be the center of my life.'"

Explore the significance of exchanging rings as outward symbols of your commitment. It is wonderful to have constant reminders of your loving promises. Historically, giving rings may have marked an actual exchange of wealth or carried overtones of ownership (read more about wedding jewelry on page 39). But in our modern society, rather than just serving as an outward sign of marriage, rings, as circles, can symbolize unending love and dedication, as well as the cycles in life and nature. Ann believes, "You don't need a ring or any material

STOP THE STOPWATCH

How long should a ceremony be? Some say, "short and sweet." Religious traditions and spiritual beliefs have their own rhythms. You can be speedy, but don't be tempted to rush it too much. This is one of the most important moments in your lives. Ann's advice on this one is: "I think a ceremony that is less than 15 or 20 minutes is too short. People need time to fully absorb what's going on. A wedding ceremony is something to relax into and focus on. Couples should understand this is a gift they're giving their guests and shouldn't feel obligated to rush through this beautiful time in their lives. Weddings offer each of us the opportunity to remember the power of loving promise."

exchange to be married, but I think a ring (or similar item) is a reminder to ourselves that we have other people we include in our decision-making. It's about saying "Here's my ring and all my dreams and promises," and for the partner to say, "Thank you, I'm going to wear this ring and cherish your love."

Part Five: Hear your marriage proclaimed and celebrate with a kiss. Call on everyone to rededicate themselves to the task of creating and supporting love in the world.

With this step, you seal the marriage. There may also be a traditional, symbolic act such as breaking a glass or jumping over a broom. Now that it's official, your celebrant says a blessing and reminds your guests — your community — of their promise to support your loving relationship.

LOCATION AND SETTING

Whenever possible, keep the ceremony and reception locations the same or in close proximity. The less complicated the transition from ceremony to reception,

SEEKING A CELEBRANT

There are many ways to involve friends or family in your celebration, even by officiating at your wedding. With some paperwork, people in many states can be legally married by a loved one ordained through ministries like the Universal Life Church <www.ulc.org>. While having an instantly ordained friend or family member as a celebrant is a non-traditional option, some couples cherish the personal connection of including someone familiar. However, before inviting someone to play such a key role, consider: Does the person present well in public? Can he or she help you craft a complete ceremony? These are two important advantages to having a professional celebrant who is trained in these matters.

Hold your ceremomy, reception, or both at a non-profit art museum. The site fees help to support cultural awareness and education, plus you can avoid the need for additional decorations, since the surroundings require no additional embellishment.

the better. Having one location cuts down on many costs including decorations, transportation costs and even the environmental costs created by shuttling groups of people from one place to another. However, it may not always be possible to have one location for everything. In those cases, consider hiring some type of group transport such as bus, trolley car, horse-drawn carriage or other means, so your guests can rely less on their own separate transportation.

Ideas for indoor ceremonies:

- A family or special church, synagogue, mosque or other religious establishment.
- Historic buildings; many times these are owned and maintained by non-profit organizations.
- Museums or other facilities belonging to non-profit organizations.
- Function rooms at a green hotel. You could start with members of the Green

Hotels Association, look for a Green Seal certified hotel, or simply talk with hotel and function room managers to learn about their measures to conserve energy, save water, and more (see page 123 for more on green hotels).

Ideas for outdoor ceremonies:

- An organic garden. Find one through Local Harvest's web site <www.localhar-vest.org>, or the Organic Trade Association <www.OTA.com>.

- On the grounds of a green hotel (see above).

- A botanical garden, nature preserve, arboretum or public park. Most cities and towns have these locations. Information can usually be located at your local government offices, on the Internet or in your local phone book. Be sure to check on any rules and regulations in place for weddings, which differ greatly from location to location.

- Seaside, beachside, lakeside, forest, meadow — some of nature's most beautiful locations, but also some of the most fragile. Ensure the location is not too ecologically sensitive, since foot and vehicle traffic from large groups can do considerable damage to fragile areas. Getting married in a pristine site to showcase your appreciation of nature is not necessarily an environmentally sound solution. If you must be married in such an area, bring the smallest number of people possible and hold a larger reception somewhere more developed.

Tips on Outdoor Ceremonies

Having a ceremony outdoors can showcase your appreciation for the environment, but there are some special considerations. First, make sure your officiant is willing to perform the ceremony at your chosen location — some will only perform wedding ceremonies within a house of worship. Many public outdoor ceremony sites will require payment to secure your reservation and may also require the

PICTURE THIS

Many couples commission calligraphers or local artists to create wedding certificates as a visible memory of their commitment to one another. Wedding certificates have been traditions for centuries in certain cultures, and are now being embraced by those who may not come from such roots. In addition to containing factual information about the celebrated event, some include the couple's vows or participation of loved ones, as with Organic Weddings' Guest Sign-In Panel (*for more information, visit* <www.organicweddings.com>).

Natural Nuptials

WENDY & D.R. — SEPTEMBER 7
THE BERKSHIRES, MASSACHUSETTS

After a romantic wedding proposal in Paris, France, complete with a custom silver and hematite engagement ring crafted by the groom, Wendy and D.R. set about planning a wedding that would incorporate their mutual concern for environmental and social issues. "A thread that runs through our careers and personal values is the desire to have a positive impact on the world," said Wendy.

would be the perfect setting for their September wedding weekend. "As a child, I went to camp there for many years and we also wanted to support a non-profit organization that shared our connection to nature," said Wendy. They announced the event using beautiful tree-free invitations on lavender-colored recycled cotton paper embedded with wildflower seeds. "Everyone thought it was so unique to be able to plant their invitation rather than just throw it away," said D.R. They also minimized their overall use of paper by forgoing ceremony programs and setting up a website to communicate other wedding information.

For wedding attire, Wendy found a sample gown made of silk. The bridesmaids found affordable, simple dresses at an online store. The groom and

Wendy and D.R., both outdoor enthusiasts, knew the charming lakeside camp, Bonnie Brae, groomsmen bought versatile, nice-quality khaki pants, dress shirts and blue blazers. ☞

Natural Nuptials

☞ The couple's gifts to the groomsmen were ties to wear with their wedding outfits. For the bridesmaids' gifts, Wendy found distinctive wool/silk shawls, made in Nepal and fairly traded through Sunrise Pashmina, a project of Bridges — Projects in Rational Tourism Development, which is dedicated to helping Nepalis find economic opportunity by valuing their natural and cultural assets.

With everyone camped out for the weekend, the couple planned fun group activities — including a Saturday morning treasure hunt for the couple's wedding rings, which had been hidden in the woods by the best man. The couple's lakeside ceremony was an inspiring mixture of readings and speeches. "We asked four important people in our lives to speak during the ceremony and focus their words on sharing stories about us, to help our guests know us better than before," explained D.R. "Many of our guests told us later it was one of the most moving wedding ceremonies they had attended." To minimize cut flowers, big pots of chrysanthemums were moved from the ceremony to the reception and later given away as gifts. Reception centerpieces consisted of water-filled bowls with ivy cuttings and floating candles.

The full-service dinner for 200 guests featured an abundance of local and natural ingredients. But the focal point of their menu was the healthful, ocean-friendly shrimp supplied by the groom's company, Green Wave Aquaculture at Harbor Branch Oceanographic Institution. The couple's array of eco-friendly wedding elements was thorough — right down to the camp's composting toilets. Their clever wedding favor, personal MagLite flashlights imprinted with the couple's wedding date and "logo," helped everyone safely find their way back to their cozy cabins after dancing long into the night.

With a weekend of wedding memories to cherish, Wendy and D.R. set off for their honeymoon in Maine's spectacular Acadia National Park. "We are big believers in our National Parks — and in the vision of our park system to protect vast areas of our country from development," Wendy said. "We couldn't think of a more perfect place to start married life." 🐦

FIND THE MEANING

Incorporating colors, herbs, flowers and other symbols into your wedding ceremony allows you to personalize your day in meaningful and memorable ways.

COLORS

- Blue — the sky, heavens, water.
- Yellow — the sun, riches.
- Brown — the earth, an important color in the cycle of life.
- Green — rebirth, vitality, nature, growth, hopefulness.
- White — light, knowledge.
- Purple — religious and spiritual color associated with rebirth.
- Red — life, energy, strength, love, passion, fire, good luck and prosperity.

AROMAS

- Invigorating — spearmint, peppermint, lime, lemon, rosemary.
- Soothing — rose, lavender, ylang-ylang, various other fresh flowers like lilies.
- Cleansing — sage, thyme, pine.
- Calming — sandalwood, frankincense, cedarwood, vanilla.

For meanings behind different flowers, visit us online at <www.organicweddings.com/flowers>.

purchase of a permit. Be sure to find out whether there are any user restrictions or activities and events conflicting with your chosen date and time. Other logistics to consider include whether or not there is ample accessibility and parking, as well as restrooms on site.

After you've chosen a site, visit it several times if possible, during the same season, day of week, and time of day as your ceremony, to get a feeling for what's in bloom as well as lighting and acoustics. Choose a specific spot and envision the ceremony occurring. This will help you think more about details and flow. If you choose a "standing room only" style ceremony, be sure to provide enough chairs for all elderly, disabled or injured individuals, and expectant mothers. No matter how short your ceremony — these people need a seat.

At an outdoor ceremony, nearly everything must be brought in, so the site should be minimally decorated. While nature can provide all the backdrop you need, if you're planning to have potted plants or freshly cut flowers, use varieties and arrangements that are tolerant to heat, humidity and wind. Try to keep them out of the sun prior to the ceremony. Natural "flowers" made of dried plant material are a perfect choice for warm-weather brides. Similar to silk flowers, these flowers look real, never wilt and can be accented with fresh greens or smaller flowers that stand up better to heat (see page 94 for more information).

LEARNING TO JUGGLE

We often describe our hectic lives as a juggling act — trying to always balance home, career, family, and more. Because of this, Ann likes to use the image of a juggler to illustrate marriage. "If I could juggle, I would do that at weddings. The three balls in the air — one for each individual and one for their relationship — illustrates perfectly that, throughout their lives, a different ball will be in ascendancy. In a healthy marriage, the cycle keeps repeating. One of the most difficult things in living out our wedding promises is the willingness to allow your partner to continue to grow. Humans resist change, but it is always with us."

A principal concern for an outdoor ceremony is how to prepare for the possibility of unpleasant weather. While rain is the most obvious concern, so is very hot and sunny weather. If you are getting married at a warm time of year, be sure you set a small amount of water aside for an emergency. Umbrellas are a considerate touch in the event of either glaring sun or pelting rain. Extreme wind can cause problems, too. Ideally, the location you've chosen will offer both indoor and outdoor options. If not, you will have to decide whether you would like to rent a tent. To plan for a blustery day, be sure anything that is lightweight is secured in some way.

Another hallmark of outdoor ceremonies, especially at dusk, can be the unappreciated arrival of biting bugs. To create a bug-free and non-toxic ceremony, use an eco-friendly bug spray without harsh chemicals or burn a few earth-smart natural citronella candles, like those from Way Out Wax <www.wayoutwax.com>.

CEREMONY PROGRAMS

Programs give you a chance to express yourself, give your guests an idea of what's to come, and thank those who have been special to your relationship or in planning your day. In the program, you can list the schedule of events and names of readings and music. Your guests will appreciate following along, and this also gives them something to do while the seats are filling up. You may want to use the program to recognize members of the wedding party or honor a deceased grandparent or other loved one. They also make a beautiful keepsake; you might coordinate the layout and printing style with your invitations. Handing out programs means using more paper, though, so you may just skip them altogether, but if you do choose to hand out programs be sure to choose a tree-free and recycled alternative. For ideas and resources on paper choices and printing methods, see page 43.

Words of Wisdom

AN INTERVIEW WITH BETSY TAYLOR, FOUNDER AND PRESIDENT, CENTER FOR A NEW AMERICAN DREAM

Betsy Taylor has gained widespread recognition for raising awareness about the damaging effects of this country's "work and spend" culture: rapid depletion of natural resources, high credit card debt, low savings, longer work weeks and frenzied families. By extolling the virtues of "More Fun, Less Stuff," Betsy's vision is to improve people's quality of life by encouraging them to stop focusing on consumption as a measure of success. Betsy sits on several charitable foundation and non-profit boards and was a member of the Population and Consumption Taskforce of the President's Council for Sustainable Development. She is the author of several books, including *What Kids Really Want That Money Can't Buy*.

Organic Weddings: Who or what shaped your life with respect to the values we see in your company and career?

Betsy Taylor: My mother, who was orphaned at age 10 and grew up on a farm with her grandparents during the Depression, was my most powerful influence. She had a clarity about what was important; she instilled in me not to be wasteful, to take care of the things you have, and to focus on the things that really matter, like family. The ethic I grew up with was about conserving things. We enjoyed nature, whether out walking or in the garden. We froze and canned food, which I still do. I've always felt connected to the land..

OW: True happiness can come from the simpler things in life, like connecting with family, friends and nature. How can busy brides and grooms reconnect with each other and those around them?

BT: First, make sure that in your day-to-day schedule, you create some space for just each other. We live in a world that's full of noise and distractions, which rewards us for constantly multi-tasking. It's important to really greet each other in the morning, to bring each other coffee or tea, and have a few minutes connecting, when you're not just reading the paper or getting out the door. It's important to be conscious about setting aside space, like eating dinner together, ☞

Words of Wisdom (contd.)

☞ because otherwise life can just be a blur. You can become roommates rather than lovers.

Second, get out into nature — it slows down the whole rhythms of our bodies as well as reconnects us. Nature is a great place to nurture human relationships. That's pretty obvious, but when 80% of Americans live in urban environments with development continuing, you have to seek it out. Find a local urban garden or bike path, or be conscious about seeing the clouds.

Third, celebrate each other's passions. Ask yourself, "What really makes me happy?" That's going to be different for different people. If one person loves dancing and the other one doesn't, try to accommodate that passion a little bit, because that's a big part of who they are at their core. Celebrate your common interests, which drew you together in the first place. Hold on to the non-material things that really jazz you and do them together.

OW: Given the environmental and social challenges of our time, how can businesses make a difference, protect the environment and promote sustainability?

BT: Our organization promotes sustainability, primarily by helping consumers find green businesses or products that are earth-friendly.

We help millions of people who want to make the world a better place through their power as consumers. No matter what the type of business, it needs to use its power to develop and promote ecological products so we can all be part of creating a sustainable future.

OW: What is something you do in your own home to reduce your ecological footprint?

BT: I have a clothesline, which I love. Even though using it takes more time, I feel my whole body slowing down because I have to go outside and be conscious of the wind and sun. I think the clothesline is one of the great, simple wonders of the world. Your clothes actually smell better and your white clothes get whiter because the sun provides a natural bleaching element.

OW: Why organic weddings?

BT: I think too many of the most special celebrations in our society, like birthdays and religious holidays, have been stolen by Madison Avenue. Having an organic wedding takes one of the most precious moments in your life and asks you not only to think about how you're going to express your love and commitment to each other, but how to do it in a way that's thoughtful and kind to the earth and those around you. It sends a message about your deepest core values. 🐚

WOW — WHY ORGANIC WEDDINGS?

It's been estimated that the ecological footprint of each modern city dweller would take up 12 acres — that's the amount of land that must be clearcut for lumber and paper, plowed for food, dammed for electric energy and irrigation, mined for coal, or otherwise interfered with to support one person. Suburban and country dwellers have an even larger footprint per person. (Source: Ernest Callenbach, *Ecology*; and Mathis Wackernagel and William Rees, *Our Ecological Footprint: Reducing Human Impact on the Earth*.)

HARMONIOUS MUSIC

Music is another wonderful way for you to bring together your love for each other and for the environment, with live instrumental pieces or vocal lyrics — performed by family members, friends or professionals. And what's the best way to go green with your wedding music and entertainment? No electricity required! Aside from the beautiful, natural sound of unplugged instruments, they don't gobble fossil fuels to operate. This usually works perfectly at ceremonies when piano, acoustic guitar, harp or chamber music set just the right tone. A cost-effective way to include live music is to hire a group from a local youth orchestra, children's choir or string quartet. Look into local non-profit organizations, music schools and other programs where you're likely to find a lot of talent at less expense. Besides sparing your budget, you are supporting the arts by encouraging these budding musicians to continue their craft. However, if live instruments aren't an option, bring along your own CDs (either store bought or your own special wedding mix) and assign someone reliable to press "play" at the right moment.

Consider using your favorite "nature sounds" recordings or beautiful seasonal and earth-inspired pieces by Vivaldi, George Winston, Windham Hill or Nature's Symphonies. If you are searching for sheet music to play or sing at your ceremony, check out *Songs for Earthlings — A Green Spirituality Songbook*, compiled and edited by Julie Forest Middleton. Another way to put some meaning into your wedding music, is with MUSE (Musicians United to Sustain the Environment) <www.musemusic.org>, an earth-friendly nonprofit group of musicians who raise money for grassroots environmental projects through CD sales and concerts. Many members of the all-volunteer group are traveling musicians, scattered around the US. They give grants to organizations dedicated to protecting endangered or threatened species and preserving existing wilderness habitats, such as the Northwest Ecosystem Alliance, the Northwoods Wilderness Recovery, and the Natural Resources Council of Maine.

CHAPTER 6

Receptions and Parties

YOUR WEDDING RECEPTION and related parties are absolutely the fun points of your nuptials. You get to relax, eat, dance and be merry. You'll also have a chance to greet your guests and thank them for celebrating with you. Your reception to-do list might seem to go on and on, but we've gathered great ideas and resources here to move your eco-planning along.

For any wedding-related party, and especially your wedding reception, begin by jotting down a timetable of events. Knowing when you want everything to happen will ensure things go like clockwork. Even if you do not intend to include traditions like throwing the bouquet or having a first dance, you should still determine when food will be served, so your caterer can be prepared.

A festive, earth-friendly reception is a goal worth striving toward, so check out our tips and tidbits. Typically, the wedding reception is the largest expenditure

Tug on anything at all and you'll find it connected to everything else in the universe.
— John Muir

in a wedding budget. So, from soup to nuts — make it organic whenever possible — and make a difference with your dollars.

SETTING AND STYLE

Formal or casual, indoors or out — these considerations all contribute to your reception or party style. It will help you establish a theme, a to-do list, and, typically, it will inspire ways to be environmentally and socially responsible. There are many types of reception venues, from your own backyard to a destination wedding across the globe. Bear in mind that more travel equals higher environmental cost; so if possible, consider a location that is convenient for your guests and near (or at the same place as) your ceremony or other events. Also, if your ceremony and reception take place during the day, you will cut down on the amount of electricity needed for lighting. If your event will be at night, save

Artfully arranged and locally grown, organic flowers grace tables covered in vintage linens.

energy by using candlelight or oil lamps and bring a soft, natural glow to your event. But remember to use care with any open flame, especially if you will have young children in attendance.

Consider the location's impact on the environment. Outdoor weddings usually require more set-up and rental items, but you benefit from Mother Nature's décor and can typically go very light on flower arrangements or other decorations. As with ceremonies, outdoor receptions should not be held in a location that is too ecologically sensitive. For more tips on outdoor events see page 63.

When possible, seek out local, privately owned businesses to help support the local economy. If dealing with larger corporations, consider their records of environmental responsibility within your community and beyond. If you are having a hotel reception, learn about their environmental stewardship practices. See page 75 for questions to ask the hotel's catering and events manager.

Be sure your clean-up crew leaves the location sparkling (without the use of harsh chemicals). In any setting, avoid using disposable products by renting all of your dishes, linens, cutlery and glassware. If you must use disposables, make sure your paper products are made from recycled paper and not virgin wood fiber. Two brands to look for are Seventh Generation and Marcal. There is even corn-based, biodgradeable cutlery now to replace plastic cutlery, which is usually non-recyclable. Recyclable plastic cups are widely available if rental glassware is not accessible. Arrange for clearly marked trash receptacles so that guests or catering staff can properly dispose of any bottles, cans or recyclable plastic.

ECO-RECEPTION BASICS

- Choose a site that supports an environmental or social cause, like a museum or an eco-hotel.
- Avoid using any disposable items. Rent any items you don't have or find them at thrift or vintage stores.
- Even if you can't find a caterer who specializes in preparing organic meals, you can work with yours to find as many organic ingredients as possible.
- Serve organic beverages such as coffee and tea. Also, consider the many types of organic wine and beer if you will have alcohol at your reception.
- Enjoy your music unplugged when possible. The sound is beautiful and doesn't require electricity — only people power.

FABULOUS FOOD

Deciding what to serve at your reception and parties can be daunting. Strive for some or all of these fabulous — and important — food statements: organic, local, fair trade, seasonal and sustainable (for more on eco-eating turn to page 148). It may be fitting to highlight specialties from your area. Many parts of the US have local specialties, such as Idaho potatoes, Washington apples, Georgia peaches and

Maine lobster. Choosing food that is grown or raised locally helps to support small and mid-size businesses with good reputations for social and environmental responsibility in their communities.

In the *Chez Panisse Menu Cookbook,* Alice Waters (interview on page 8) advises: "There is nothing simpler or more economical than buying what is in season — if you know what is in season. Unfortunately, going to the supermarket, which tries to supply all of the produce all of the time, and looking at waxed and treated fruit will not give you the answer … Learning comes from critically tasting and evaluating the produce on a month-to-month basis … For me, the seasons are the starting points. I just pick and choose foods for a menu guided by the stimuli of perfectly ripe tomatoes, succulent spring lamb, a new garlic harvest, or fragrant fresh basil." To guide your special event (and day-to-day) menu planning adventures, turn to page 159 for Chez Panisse's Seasonal Foods Calendar.

Have fun planning your menu and remember, it's a shame to let extra food, organic or not, go to waste. So, discuss with your caterer (or hotel catering manager) how to donate any leftovers to a local homeless shelter or food bank. Be sure to make arrangements well in advance so the staff is prepared to properly wrap up any donations. Contact your local homeless shelter or food bank for guidelines on food donation. Second Harvest <www.secondharvest.org> is the nation's largest domestic hunger relief organization, with a network of over 200 food banks and food-rescue programs.

Choosing a Caterer:

QUESTIONS TO ASK

- Will all drinks, including soda be served in glass (not plastic)?

- Will the drinks served outside also be served in glass (not plastic)?

- Will the bar have fountain soda, water and tonic water or be stocked with individual containers?

- Will the water served to guests at the bar be tap or bottled water?

- If we want organic wines and beers, will your distributor have access to those products?

- During the cocktail hour will non-disposable plates be made available for crudite, cheese and fruit platters?

- Will your staff know which hors d'oeuvres are vegetarian/vegan and which are not?

- Are the paper napkins you serve with drinks made from recycled materials?

- Do you collect and sort your disposables (glass, plastic, metal)?

- Do you donate leftover food to a local shelter or organization that collects it for the hungry?

- Do you use organic dairy, vegetables, meat, dry or frozen organic ingredients?

- Will there be a price premium for organic ingredients?

- Do you use locally grown or produced ingredients?

- Will there be a price premium for local ingredients?

- Do you have experience cooking vegetarian or vegan foods?

- Does your kitchen cook non-meat items separate from meat items, for example on the grill and for deep fried foods?

- Do you avoid serving seafood that is in the "red" zone on the Seafood Watch List for this region?

- Do you buy meat products from farms that raise their animals naturally?

- Do you serve fair trade and organic coffees and teas?

Q & A

What is the best way to include local, organic food in our winter wedding? We live in the Midwest and will be way past our local growing season.

In many parts of the country, a winter wedding can make finding organic and locally grown ingredients a challenge. The cost of shipping fresh organic produce from warmer regions might be beyond your budget. In these cases, work with your caterer to determine if there are any winter greenhouses in the area growing organic lettuces or other produce. Beyond that, many non-perishable items in your meal can be organic. For example, serve only organic beverages: coffee, tea, juice, wine and beer. Organic dry ingredients like sugar, pasta and flour are easy to find and store. Organic frozen items may be an option, too, depending on your menu and your freezer storage facilities. All of these items can be purchased ahead of time and brought or shipped directly to your caterer or reception location.

Meat, Poultry and Seafood Options

If you decide to serve beef, chicken, turkey or other meat at your wedding, ensure that the animals have been raised humanely and on organic feed, without the use of hormones and other chemicals. Additionally, the farms should be clean and properly manage their waste disposal. In the US, large-scale animal factory farming has a poor record of environmental responsibility and concern for animal welfare. Fortunately, availability of naturally raised meat is growing. Check your local health food markets for possible sources. However, even with naturally raised meat, there are still environmental costs. According to *The Better World Handbook*, "About one-fourth of the Earth's land is used to graze cattle. A reduced demand for meat would mean we could use this land to raise grain, which would feed more people with greater efficiency, and we would help to protect the world's grasslands from overgrazing." So, when serving meat at your wedding or other parties, consider minimizing the total amount of meat used by including lots of delicious vegetarian and vegan dishes.

There are important considerations if you will be serving fish and seafood. Seafood Watch Lists are divided among three categories: Best Choice, Proceed with Caution and Avoid. Check current lists from either the Monterey Bay

Aquarium <www.mbayaq.org/cr/seafoodwatch.asp> or Audubon Society <www.audubon.org/campaign/lo/seafood/> to ensure that the fish you serve is not in the Avoid category. Species are placed in this category due to overfishing of wild populations or because they are caught or farmed in ways that harm the environment. The lists are regularly updated based on information from many fishery organizations around the world.

Vegetarian and Vegan Options

Vegetarian and vegan diets are increasingly popular for many reasons including health, ethical, religious and environmental concerns. Diets without meat or animal products require more thoughtful menu planning, but with the scores of vegetarian and vegan cookbooks on the market, even a novice can prepare a gourmet meal. The Internet-savvy will find no shortage of great web sites offering a wide variety of vegetarian and vegan wedding menus, recipes and links. These should provide you or your caterer with many possibilities for meat-free wedding meals.

If the bride and groom are meat-eaters and will serve a meat entrée, it is considerate and appropriate to offer an alternative vegetarian or vegan entrée. This is even more the case if serving beef, since even some non-vegetarians have stopped eating red meat for health or other reasons. The same is true for hors d'oeuvres and appetizers. Always offer meat-free alternatives. Vegetarians and vegans have chosen to restrict their diets for reasons that are important to them. Be inclusive and sensitive to these convictions. You might also consider serving raw foods, such as fruits, nuts, vegetables and sprouted grains. They are refreshing and healthful, and fewer natural resources are used when growing and preparing them. Chances are, if you care enough to plan an

"*We* arranged many small pre-wedding lunches among people so they got to know each other. For example, there was a men's lunch with fathers, brothers, groomsmen, and so on. There were also two ladies' lunches with different groups of people: mothers, sisters, bridesmaids and cousins. All that female energy at the ladies' lunches was a great calming influence. We had also arranged for various people to give each other a lift to the wedding location, so the lunches helped them get to know each other." — *Elise*

This gorgeous wedding cake illustrates that going organic can be very stylish. The cake is made from 100% organic ingredients; the flowers are also organic.

earth-friendly wedding, many of your guests are eco-conscious or are at least aware of your concern for the environment. As a result, everyone, even if they are not vegetarians, will appreciate your thoughtful menu decisions.

Looking for a less formal dinner than the traditional sit-down affair, but not ready for long buffet lines? Try a compromise that is usually less expensive than a seated dinner, but has the eco-benefit of minimizing leftovers better than buffets. Family-style or banquet dining, where guests share platters of each course brought to their tables, is less service-intensive and more relaxed than a formal dinner service.

The Wedding Cake

Having a delicious and beautiful organic wedding cake is not as difficult as it may sound. In most cases, traditional recipes can be used, unlike with vegan wedding cakes. Our online Resources Directory lists organic bakers, some of which also bake organic vegan cakes. (Visit <www.organicweddings.com/resources>.)

If you are searching for an organic baker, but can't locate one, ask a conventional baker if they are willing to purchase organic and natural ingredients for your cake. Even if only half of the ingredients can be organic, go for it. Half is better than none. You may find a baker who is interested in helping you and in learning to source ingredients for an organic cake. Local health and natural food stores in your area should carry necessary baking products.

Organic flowers (choose edible if they will stay on when served) or ribbons are great ideas for wedding cake decorations, rather than the cheap plastic or metal cake toppers commonly used. The petroleum-based plastic columns, arches and figurines are usually non-recyclable and end up being thrown away. If you must have a cake topper, visit a local antique store for something vintage or purchase a porcelain or similar item that you will cherish as an heirloom.

ORGANIC BEVERAGES

A wide range of organic and natural beverages is available to serve your guests, including coffee, tea, juice, wine and beer. No matter what you consider appropriate beverages for your event, there are organic choices you'll enjoy. Check our online Resources Directory <www.organicweddings.com/resources> to find companies providing all types of organic beverages.

Natural Nuptials

KATHY AND BRETT — OCTOBER 12
NORTHERN CALIFORNIA

*K*athy and Brett are both at home in the outdoors and met while working at a summer camp in California. They share a love of world-wide hiking adventures and together have climbed peaks from Alaska to Nepal. So, it was fitting that the couple got engaged on Valentine's Day, at sunset, atop the third largest pyramid in the world — the Pyramid of the Sun, outside of Mexico City. A cocktail reception for a conference they were attending that night turned into their impromptu engagement party, complete with an unforgettable serenade by a Mexican band covering Beatles songs while dressed in full Sgt. Pepper regalia.

Kathy's event-planning experience and

her love of the environment came together for her sunflower-themed organic wedding in Northern California's Gold Country. "I was getting absolutely fed up with looking at all the wedding magazines that promote excess, synthetics, and nothing close to being eco-friendly." So, Kathy took matters into her own capable hands and together with her fiancé and helpful friends, planned an incredible eco-wedding.

To announce their special event, Kathy, a talented artist, created a sunflower drawing for their wedding invitations, which were printed on tree-free and recycled paper. For both their ceremony and reception, the couple chose a local non-profit organization's retreat center.

Natural Nuptials

☞ "Having everything in one spot also minimized transportation needs," said Brett. Flowers were abundant, but there wasn't a pesticide-sprayed rose in sight. Kathy had the help of a local organic farmer who provided a bounty of seasonal blooms that were transformed into spectacular floral archways, bouquets and centerpieces. Three days before the ceremony, Kathy visited a beloved natural site, the South Yuba River, for inspiration to write her vows. "It didn't take long before the words flowed right out onto paper ... the river was a perfect place to center my excited self," she said. Kathy's appreciation stems in part from her work to help preserve this beautiful river through the South Yuba River Citizens League.

Amid scenic grounds, an expansive organic potluck banquet was laid out for 325 guests. In addition to the grilled free-range chicken provided by the bride and groom, guests brought along their best organic cooking to share. Dishes included everything from Indian curry to Italian pasta. Even the beverages were organic, including organic wines from California and Italy, as well as Wolavers' organic beer. There was, of course, an organic wedding cake. You might think that after such decadence, the guests would be stuck in their seats, but the local cover band got everyone dancing under clear skies and twinkling stars.

When catering to such a large group, the use of plastic and paper disposables can be tempting, but not for this eco-couple. All dinnerware, glasses and other serving needs were rented. Recycled vases, obtained from local secondhand stores, and vintage fabrics made festive decorations for the party. For her wedding ensemble, Kathy found a vintage eyelet lace skirt for which she had a local seamstress create a coordinating eyelet bodice. The bridesmaids and flower girl all wore colorful hemp dresses from Ecolution. Not to be outdone, the men — from the groom to the ring bearer — wore festive organic cotton shirts from Patagonia.

The blissful couple topped off their celebration with a week-long honeymoon at a friend's vacation home on the famously spectacular Hawaiian island of Kauai, where they spent time hiking along the island's breathtaking coastline. ☙

Organic/Fair Trade Coffee and Tea

The US is the largest importer of coffee in the world, which is not surprising if you consider that Americans spend $18 billion a year on coffee. Unfortunately, coffee beans are exported mainly from countries where organic farming and fair trade practices are not widespread. Because of this, a handful of companies have worked hard to support small scale, organic farmers who are growing coffee beans naturally, without degrading the environment. In exchange for their stewardship, these smaller farmers are receiving fair prices for their beans, giving them a road out of extreme poverty.

Serving organic coffee and/or tea at your reception and other wedding parties is an easy way to bring both environmental and social awareness to your events. Not only does organic coffee and tea taste better than the stuff sprayed with chemicals, but by choosing organic and fairly-traded products, you are voicing your concern for farmers' quality of life in developing countries throughout Latin America, Asia and Africa.

If you are having a hard time finding an organic caterer in your area, or if you would like to incorporate something earth-friendly and you're already in the later planning stages, organic tea or coffee is an easy choice. You can mail-order or buy these products in advance, and give them to your caterer to prepare and serve on your wedding day. Last, but not least, when you serve your delicious and socially responsible coffee and tea, don't forget the proper accompaniments — organic milk, honey, sugar and lemons — all easy-to-find organic products.

Organic Wine and Beer

If you are planning to serve beer or wine at your reception or wedding-related parties, use this as another opportunity to support organic products. Organic beverages have even expanded to include vodka.

" *We* had a brunch for over 100 people at my parents' house the morning after the wedding. We wanted it to be low stress and minimize the work, but felt strongly about not using disposables. We ended up negotiating a great price for renting linens, utensils, plates, coffee mugs and carafes. Not only did we reduce the amount of waste we generated, but it was a nice touch. While planning my wedding, I found if I explained to people that I was trying to be environmentally-conscious, they were willing to help me out more because, by association, it got them involved in doing good, too." — *Jaime*

Organic wine is made from grapes grown without the use of synthetic fertilizers, pesticides or other chemicals, all of which can damage soil and water, while ending up in the wine as residue. Organic wine can also encompass the production process and whether or not sulfites and other preservatives have been added. If you are planning to serve wine at your reception and related parties, go organic. You may even find a sparkling wine that suits your taste and can be used in place of champagne for your wedding toasts.

If you have difficulty locating organic wines, consider supporting a conventional winery that is making progress towards environmental sustainability. For example, Kendall-Jackson Wine Estates uses integrated pest management in most of its vineyards, and even received an EPA award in 2002 for its efforts to reduce the ozone-depleting chemical methyl bromide. Or consider Fetzer Vineyards: with over 2,000 organic vineyard acres, the company has committed to grow and purchase 100% organic grapes by 2010.

Words of Wisdom

AN INTERVIEW WITH
BARNEY FEINBLUM, PRESIDENT
AND CEO, ORGANIC VINTNERS

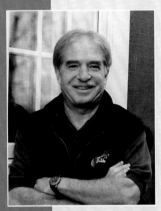

From tea to milk to wine, Barney Feinblum's career is nearly overflowing with organic beverages. His previous CEO positions at the helm of natural products giants Celestial Seasonings and Horizon Organic Dairy have given him a perspective that few share. He not only led the management group that re-acquired Celestial from Kraft Foods in 1988, but also led Horizon in their 1998 initial public offering. A few years ago, he founded Organic Vintners to import notable organic wines from around the world. A native of Brooklyn, New York, Barney has made his home in Boulder, Colorado, for over 30 years and now serves as a Director for natural products companies Gaiam, Seventh Generation, Fresh and Wild, and Pharmaca.

Organic Weddings: Who or what shaped your life with respect to the values we see in your company and career?

Barney Feinblum: I'm a product of the 60s; my values were set as a student at Cornell University. In those days we got involved in the issues, for example civil rights and women's lib. The environmental movement was a product of that group of people looking for more selfless answers to how they should relate to the planet.

The slogan that most inspired me from those days was, "If you're not part of the solution, you're part of the problem." So I set out to be part of the solution and got involved with companies that were doing good things; that is what eventually led me to work at Celestial Seasonings, and to other opportunities within the natural products industry. I thought it was a great industry, full of people who were committed to a double bottom line. Most of them at that time didn't think they'd be running successful businesses. Yet, they ended up doing just that because they were committed to their values and to building wonderful companies.

OW: Couples who serve organic products when entertaining family and friends help to build demand for healthy and environmentally friendly goods. For many, the benefits of ☞

Words of Wisdom (contd.)

☞   buying locally are apparent, but what are the benefits of supporting global organic agriculture?

BF: We're all in one world. Most people enter the organic movement for some reason or value that is important to them. Soon, you begin to realize that there is a whole lifestyle of products and ways you can contribute to make this a better planet.

Whether it is internationally produced herb tea, domestic organic dairy products or imported organic wine, you are part of this international organic community that is really changing the planet. By consuming these products, we help more and more acres of farmland to be converted to organic worldwide. We should buy locally when we can, but a lot of things don't grow in the climates nearby. The most important thing is to commit to an organic lifestyle and support the people who are committed to providing those products around the globe.

OW: Given the environmental and social challenges of our time, how can businesses make a difference, protect the environment and promote sustainability?

BF: Business crosses national and therefore governmental boundaries. People vote with their wallets by supporting good companies, and as a result they are doing their part to help change the world. We've made major progress in the past 25 years; organic food accounts for less than 1.5% of all food, but with growth rates of over 20% that number will increase to 5-10% over the next decade.

OW: What is something you do in your own home to reduce your ecological footprint?

BF: My wife and I designed our own home back in the 70s. We started by not building an enormous house and also built it for passive solar with lots of south-facing glass. We eat all organic foods, use environmentally friendly cleaning products and recycle everything. We like to find our entertainment in the outdoors with lots of camping and hiking.

OW: Why organic weddings?

BF: I can't think of a more wonderful statement to make about what is important to you, your life and the family you are about to create. You also aren't sacrificing to do it. Thirty years ago, you might not have been able to have a fancy catered meal, elegant flowers or nice invitations, but that's all changed. It joyously shows how you intend to make a difference. ❧

Organic beer has made strides in recent years to improve taste while using organically grown hops, malts, barleys, and natural yeast, as well as cutting out chemical additives. The industry is growing and so are the number of great offerings from breweries like Wolaver's, Crannog Ale and Pacific Western Breweries.

MUSIC AND ENTERTAINMENT

While the eco-friendly sounds of piano, acoustic guitar, harp or chamber music may work perfectly at your ceremony and cocktail hour, you may be looking for something a bit snappier to get the party started later on. What's an eco-minded couple to do? If your wedding reception is large, you may need to go the traditional route with a DJ or hire a local band. Another option for reception and party music is to mix your own CDs and assign someone to play them continuously through the evening. Admittedly, this idea works better in smaller venues. Remember, part of planning an organic wedding is striking a balance. Strive to do what you can, where and when you can. Even if you aren't always able to go green for everything, any earth-friendly choice is a step in the right direction. If you have many guests and enough space, consider hiring a small orchestra. Even if the orchestra opts to have speakers, overall they will be playing instruments that do not require electricity; and that big band sound will inspire guests of all ages to dance the night away.

WOW — WHY ORGANIC WEDDINGS?

Currently only about 3.5% of all plastics generated are recycled, compared to 34% of paper, 22% of glass and 30% of metals. At this time, plastics recycling only minimally reduces the amount of virgin resources used to make plastics. Recycling paper, glass and metal — materials that are easily recycled more than once — saves far more energy and resources than are saved with plastics recycling. So, when you have an alternative choice available, limit your plastic consumption as much as possible. (Source: <www.eco-cycle.org>.)

ZERO WASTE AND RENEWABLE ENERGY

Take your reception to the next level by making it a zero waste event and powering it with clean energy. You'll do great things for the environment by reducing the amount of trash created and building more demand for renewable energy.

The bride is wearing a
square neck hemp/silk ball
gown with a silk shawl.

The bride is wearing
a two-piece hemp/silk
ensemble with a bias
cut skirt, scoop neck
bodice and peplum.
The groom is wearing
a hemp outfit from
Sweetgrass Natural Fibers.

*T*he bride is wearing
an empire waist hemp/silk
gown with a detachable silk
gauze train. The groom's
hemp/silk vest is coupled with
an antique cotton dress shirt.

*T*he bride and
her daughter wear
coordinating
hemp/silk dresses.

The bride is wearing
a strapless hemp/silk
bridal gown.

The bride is wearing an
empire waist hemp/silk
gown with a silk gauze overskirt.

*P*lace cards made by recycling the bride & groom's own junk mail..

A handcrafted bouquet of natural Cream roses with organic floral accents..

*I*vy cuttings in water with floating candles illuminate the table.

*O*rganic flowers and ingredients make for a beautiful cake, like this one from Petite Patisserie in San Francisco, CA.

To make your wedding reception a zero waste event takes commitment in the planning stages. Avoid all disposable items and excess packaging, and set up well-marked receptacles to assist your guests or catering staff in separating out their recyclables. Finally, at the end of the event, a few people should be available to take disposables to be recycled or stored properly until pick-up. Creating a zero waste event is extra work, but the results are well worth the effort.

Power Your Wedding with Wind

Create a zero pollution event by replacing the electricity you draw from the national grid with clean, renewable energy. According to the Union of Concerned Scientists, just two percent of our nation's electricity comes from clean, sustainable sources like wind, solar and other renewable technologies. Yet, the US is blessed with enough renewable resources to meet more than 4.5 times current electricity needs. A California-based company called 3 Phases Energy sells Green Certificates, which represent watts of clean energy produced on wind farms. Effectively, you can balance out the pollution of ordinary power generation, sparing the environment from coal, oil, nuclear or gas emissions and mining damage. You'll also support the growth of the renewable energy market, which is improving air quality and helping to revitalize rural communities. The beauty of this simple exchange is that even though most local utilities don't offer a "green power" option, you can create exactly the same benefits through renewable certificates as you would by directly using renewable energy.

"When I was looking at hotels for our reception, I started by asking three questions: Are you a Green Hotel? Do you use any locally grown or produced ingredients in your restaurant? Do you donate your leftover food to feed the hungry? After I choose my reception location, I wrote to the other locations that answered "no" to any of those questions and let them know that it had contributed to my decision not to hold my reception there." — *Tracey*

How does it work? 3 Phases Energy <www.3phases.com> can give you a customized estimate of how much renewable, wind-generated energy it will take to balance out your reception. Factors will include the number of guests, whether your event will be held indoors or outdoors, whether you're having

Words of Wisdom

AN INTERVIEW WITH NORA POUILLON, FOUNDER AND CHEF, RESTAURANT NORA AND ASIA NORA

*N*ora Pouillon, pioneer organic chef and restaurant owner, opened Washington, DC's Restaurant Nora in 1979. Since then, she has been a vocal advocate of healthy, organic living, serving only food that is seasonal and fresh. In April 1999, Restaurant Nora became the first certified organic restaurant in the country. Her second restaurant, Asia Nora, features healthy dishes from cuisines across Asia. Nora has written a cookbook, *Cooking With Nora,* and is involved in numerous programs to support organic agriculture.

Organic Wedings: Who or what shaped your life with respect to the values we see in your company and career?

Nora Pouillon: My parents were very health-conscious; we ate very — whole grains, lots of fruit and vegetables — and we spent a lot of time outdoors, enjoying nature. Another influence was the French school in Vienna·I attended for 10 years. Every day we sat down to a three course lunch of French cuisine. The cooking part for me came later. I discovered a book on French cooking by Elizabeth David, which became my bible. She emphasized cooking methods that don't destroy nutritional value, as well as the importance of fresh, pure ingredients. She also balanced ingredients across the meal and spoke a lot about regional specialties and seasonal eating, advising where and when to buy the best ingredients.

OW: What element of your work do you most enjoy?

NP: I enjoy the creativity and the freedom to change the menu every day. I also really enjoy encouraging people to perhaps be more daring in their food choices. My menu represents all types of taste buds. Everything is inspiring; nothing is routine.

OW: As the founder of the first certified organic restaurant in the US, how do you approach educating your clientele about the benefits of organic food?

NP: I do as much as I can without sounding too preachy. I include information all over my menu. I spend my energy educating and informing people because many people don't think ☞

Words of Wisdom (contd.)

☛ of the quality of food — where it has come from or how it was grown. They think about low fat or fresh versus frozen, but they don't think about conventional versus organic. I also list all the vegetables and fruit, and even the fish that are currently in season.

OW: **Given the environmental and social challenges of our time, how can businesses make a difference, protect the environment and promote sustainability?**

NP: We compost all of our vegetable trimmings, and I use the soil created from this compost in my organic garden. It's such beautiful, dark, rich soil. We also sort and recycle our plastics and glass. The uniform shirts are 100% organic cotton, and our carpet is biodegradable and recycled. We use non-VOC paints, so they don't give off toxic fumes. Whenever we find out about something that's better, we research it and try to implement it.

We are proud of the fact that we support and encourage farmers to convert to organics. When I opened in 1976 there were not many organic farmers; I had to ask people to become organic and be my suppliers. I told them I'd buy every animal they raised as long as they were raised without any hormones or antibiotics;

or I'd buy all the tomatoes if they didn't use any pesticides. In the last 5-10 years, people started coming to me who had farms that were becoming organic but were not yet certified asking if I was interested in buying from them. I told them yes, but they first needed their organic certification. For instance, the woman who grows my risotto came to me about 10 years ago. She had a big rice farm in California but it wasn't yet certified organic. I suggested that if she became certified organic, she might try growing risotto rice. She called me up three years later and said, "I have your organic risotto."

OW: Why organic weddings?

NP: Be an example, so people will see what you've done, and how you live, and how you planned your wedding. If you knew fully how conventional food is grown and raised and about the impact it has on the health of this planet and future generations, you would not support it. Think about all the health problems we have — it's like a snowball that starts out small and by the end of the day it's enormous. So if you make these little differences and don't let the snowball get going, it won't have the chance to get bigger. 🐚

" *We* chose a family-run inn for our reception. We also chose locally brewed beer and other regional specialties. Keeping money in the local area of our wedding and supporting independently owned businesses were two of our goals." — *Amy*

amplified music at the reception, and heating or cooling requirements. For an average wedding, the cost of making your event renewable would be around 45 cents per guest. You can post the certificate you receive at the reception, make an announcement, or simply mention in your wedding program that your day is "powered by renewable energy." You can also purchase certificates to offset wedding travel or your day-to-day household use. Another company offering similar services is Renewable Choice Energy <www.renewablechoice.com>. Even small events contribute important visibility and momentum to the renewable energy movement. So build awareness at your wind-powered wedding and help create a cleaner, greener future.

CHAPTER 7

Delightful Details

A SAYING GOES, "THE DEVIL IS IN THE DETAILS"; but when planning an organic wedding, we believe the *delight* is in the details because this is where you can find countless unique and stylish opportunities to infuse your environmental and social values into your wedding day. Favors, flowers, gifts and more offer you many options for personalizing your wedding, while remaining environmentally and socially responsible.

THE POWER OF FLOWERS

With wedding flowers, brides have a significant chance to make more conscientious decisions. Many of the flowers sold by florists and supermarket floral departments have been imported from developing countries where pesticide use is very high and labor wages are very low. Unfortunately, pesticide regulations

> "
> Those who contemplate the beauty of the earth find reserves of strength that will endure as long as life lasts.
> — Rachel Carson

"*I* wanted organic, locally grown flowers for my late-fall wedding, but none of the florists in the area were interested in helping me because it would be just past the local growing season. I approached a woman selling flowers at a local farmer's market about doing dried bouquets and arrangements from her summer flowers that dried well. She had never done a wedding before but was really excited to have the opportunity. Everything looked beautiful and very unique!" —*Danielle*

are not as stringent overseas as they are in the US and Canada. As a result, many imported cut flowers have been sprayed with toxic chemicals to keep them cosmetically perfect. These chemicals are not only toxic to us, but do great environmental damage in the countries where the flowers are cultivated. The chemicals are related to health problems experienced by the people, mostly women, who cultivate these flowers and are exposed to much higher quantities of these toxins than is safe. Cut flowers are expensive and get thrown away quickly. Consequently, we suggest finding alternatives and compromises to the traditional use of wedding flowers.

Organic and Local

Use only organic flowers, locally grown and in season, if possible. If you are thinking of using local wildflowers, please be careful and resist picking your own. Wildflowers are fragile, as is the environment that nurtures them. Leave wildflowers to reseed. If you want to use wildflowers for your wedding, please buy them from a grower who cultivates them organically. Furthermore, some wildflowers are actually flowering weeds to which many people are allergic, so be sure to avoid those in your arrangements.

If you like to garden or have a friend with a green thumb, consider growing some or even all of your own wedding flowers. This project needs to be started about two to four months ahead of time, but can yield beautiful bouquets of totally organic homegrown flowers. If your wedding isn't taking place during the local outdoor growing season, consider forcing bulbs. A variety of species such as tulips, daffodils, crocuses, hyacinths, irises, and lilies-of-the-valley can be grown by this method, which involves tricking the bulbs into thinking they have spent a frosty winter underground and are ready to send up their spring blooms. You'll need to consult a timetable for each flower's chilling and growing times. We recommend reading Katherine Whiteside's book, *Forcing, Etc.* for some basic guidelines. Finding organic bulbs can take some searching, but a good place to start online is at TulipWorld <www.tulipworld.com>, which sells "ECO bulbs" grown under strict European organic standards. If you are interested in choosing flowers with symbolic meaning, visit us online at <www.organicweddings.com>.

Reduce and Reuse

Reuse the same flowers on your wedding day by arranging to have your ceremony flowers moved to your reception location. The next day, ask someone from your wedding party to donate them to a local hospital or nursing home, where your special flowers can be appreciated by many more (call ahead first for any guidelines that may exist). Use potted plants as centerpieces or accents, instead of cut flowers. Potted plants are more earth-friendly since they can be used indoors or replanted outside if kept or given away. To save money, potted plants can even be rented. Check out your local yellow pages for a florist or rental company near you.

Cut down on the amount of flowers used at your wedding by forgoing boutonnieres and corsages in favor of fabric flowers, or vintage pins with ribbons in your wedding colors that can be given as treasured gifts. You can also simplify table centerpiece designs 'so fewer cut flowers are

*F*lowers can serve as more than just decoration. Make them meaningful by honoring a loved one with some of his or her favorite flowers incorporated into your bouquet. Or, instead of buying two corsages, place two extra flowers in the bridal bouquet, for the bride to present to her mother and mother-in-law.

needed. Non-flower centerpieces, like floating candles in a glass dish with ivy cuttings, are distinctive and eye-catching. The ivy can then be taken home and rooted easily as a nice wedding memento. However, ivy should remain an indoor plant to avoid having it overrun native plants. Some brides and bridesmaids are using bouquets made of jewelry wire, translucent ribbons and crystal beads. These unique alternatives have the benefit of never fading and are especially eye-catching at evening or candlelit ceremonies. Bee Natural <www.beenatural.com> has a 100 percent beeswax "Honeypot" with pressed natural flowers that makes another great alternative to cut flower arrangements. These unique Honeypots also have votive candles inside, so are a nice option for evening receptions.

Use only seasonal items as decorations. For example, autumn weddings in colder regions can feature chrysanthemums, apples, ornamental gourds, berries, branches tied with ribbons and autumn leaves. In winter, use a stylish variety of evergreens. You can get a head start by getting married during a holiday or festive time of year, so wherever you marry will already be decorated. This cuts down on waste and costs.

Dried and Silk

"*T*o avoid cut flower centerpieces, we used small potted plants in pretty ceramic blue and white pots with a combination of green and flowering plants. There were four potted plants per table at a cost of about $32 per table; $16 for the plants and $16 for the pots. We also encouraged guests to take them home as a living reminder of our wedding."

— *Jessica*

Use dried local (organic, if possible) flowers for a creative bouquet. Choose varieties that still look good when dried and are sturdy, such as statice, pussy willow or straw flowers. Accent a dried bouquet with the fragrance of fresh organic herbs such as rosemary, then wrap with raffia or a ribbon. Two sources for dried flowers are: the Women's Organic Flower Enterprise <www.homelessgardenproject.org/wofe.html>, a program helping homeless and low-income women; and Keuka Flower Farm <www.driedflowersdirect.com>, a small family-owned farm in New York's Finger Lakes Region. Or, choose silk flowers. Silk flowers have become so realistic in recent years that most people will not be able to tell the difference from even a short distance. Silk flowers are a good choice for outdoor summer weddings where a few hours of heat will make your bouquets and boutonnieres look downright droopy. Roses are especially notorious for wilting fast on hot days. Bouquets can be made up in advance, allowing you to be sure of your choices. The quality of silk flowers does vary, so be sure to examine them ahead of time. Choose real silk flowers, which are made from a renewable resource, and not synthetic fabric or plastic ones, which are petroleum-based.

Tiny tree saplings create excellent favors.

FUN WITH FAVORS

The possibilities for creative, earth-friendly favors are boundless. Have fun with this part of your wedding planning and send your guests off in eco-style. Get creative; there's something for every budget and theme.

Trees, Seeds and More

Give the gift of oxygen with seedlings or tree seed kits as wedding favors. Trees fight global warming, help conserve energy, prevent soil erosion and clean the air. For these reasons and more, tree saplings make wonderful and meaningful favors. By the time you celebrate your silver anniversary, your wedding guests will have nurtured a small forest of carbon-dioxide-eating green beauties. Sources for saplings include: The National Arbor Day Foundation <www.arbor-day.org/gifttrees>, Evergreen Memories <www.evergreenmemories.ca>, or The GreenWorld Project <www.greenworldproject.net>. Or check out the Tree in a Box seed kit with personalized wedding labels <www.treeinabox.com>.

This bride and groom chose wooden bread baskets as their functional and unique centerpieces. The bowls, carved by the groom's talented uncle, were filled with assorted bread by the caterer and later given away as thank you gifts.

Use unique handmade papers, like Organic Weddings' Wildflowers to Go paper for favors (or invitations) that will grow. This paper is made from recycled cotton and has wildflower seeds scattered throughout. The paper can double as place cards as well as thank you favors at every guest's seat. When your guests return home and water their favors (while the seeds germinate) the wildflowers will sprout from the card.

Give each wedding guest the present of a packet of certified organic seeds from Seeds of Change <www.seedsofchange.com>. The company is a recognized leader in sustainable agriculture. More ideas for plantable favors include ornamental seed pods made from hand-molded paper in the shape of hearts, butterflies, or snowflakes and filled with flower seeds, from Favors by Serendipity <www.favorsbyserendipity.com> and Plant a Memory <www.plantamemory.com>. Your guests can admire them hanging in a window at home, or plant them and think of you whenever they see the flowers that have grown.

Items like Frisbees, cups and pens made from recycled materials such as currency, denim and newspaper, are available from Direct Access International <www.directaccessintl.com>. These fun items can be imprinted with your name and wedding date.

Finding Flowers:

QUESTIONS TO ASK

If your flowers are coming from an organic farm:

- What types of flowers do you regularly grow?

- What is in season at the time of the wedding?

- Which flowers can be successfully dried?

- Have you ever grown flowers for a wedding or another big event? If so, was it successful?

- Will you grow certain flowers on special request?

- What is your policy if the flowers grown on special request do not bloom at the right time or become infested with pests?

- Do you need a deposit for seeds or bulbs?

- Who is going to pick the flowers and when?

- Who will arrange the flowers?

- How much will this cost?

- Do you deliver? How far? What is the charge?

If your flowers are coming from a traditional florist:

- Do you buy any flowers from local farms?

- Do you buy any organic flowers for bouquets and other arrangements?

- Do you buy organic flowers for cake toppers?

- Are your flowers locally grown or shipped in from other states or abroad?

- Do you know anything about the conditions under which the flowers are grown?

- What types of chemicals do you use on the flowers once they are in your shop?

- What kinds of precautions are made here in the shop to protect the people who work with the flowers?

- Can we avoid plastic flower holders and other disposable items in our arrangements?

"*Wedding* favors were an aspect of our wedding that I hated thinking about. We could not seem to come up with anything original and I couldn't think of a time I even remembered bringing a wedding favor home. Donating to a charity, however, seemed like a thoughtful, useful and meaningful wedding favor. My younger sister is a cancer survivor so we decided to donate money in each person's name to the National Childhood Cancer Foundation. We put the information on the backs of each person's place card. There are so many different charities and most have websites that tell you how to donate and exactly what your donation goes toward."

— *Andrea*

"*Instead* of party favors, we donated $5 per guest to the Nature Conservancy for conservation of land in a place that holds special meaning for us. They printed up beautiful cards saying that a donation had been made in the name of (blank) to preserve the land. We filled in our guests' names and left them on the tables. We were amazed and gratified by how well this was received." — *Jessica*

Sweet Eats

If you are looking for a cozier touch at a smaller wedding, why not make your own organic cookie favors? Use your favorite cookie recipe and buy all organic ingredients. Get your bridal party together to help out. Tie your cookies up in little recycled paper bags or boxes and hand them out with handwritten notes of thanks on decorative tree-free paper hang tags.

For those of you who can't resist the sweet smell of chocolate, you'll find organic options are plentiful. A number of companies offer organic chocolate, like Dagoba Chocolates <www.dagobachocolate.com> and Chocolate Necessities <www.chocolatenecessities.com>. Jubilee Chocolates <www.jubilee-chocolates.com>, while not 100% certified organic, is recognized for their involvement in the community, sourcing some ingredients locally, such as mint leaves grown by youngsters at the Drew Elementary School in Philadelphia, PA. When checking out any chocolate, remember there are fair trade issues associated with cocoa. So, if you aren't sure, ask the company for assurance that their cocoa is sourced responsibly. Organic baked goods make great favors and can be shipped or picked up the week of your wedding and still stay fresh. Some cookies even help the homeless, like the Dancing Deer Bakery's Sweet Home Project. Visit our Resources Directory <www.organicweddings.com/resources> to find a bakery in your area.

Heavenly Herbs

While rosemary will always be famous for symbolizing remembrance, lavender is one of the most heavenly herbs around. Known for its magical power of relaxation, what bride couldn't benefit from having a bit of on-site aromatherapy for the big day? Lavender Green <www.lavendergreen.-com> has created a beautiful collection of wedding accessories using their organic lavender. For the do-it-yourselfer, make up little bags of fresh or dried organic herbs to hand out as favors. If you're serving a favorite dish at your reception (that calls for spices or herbs), hand out small packets of the pre-measured

"*Rather* than decorating the tables with flower centerpieces, we used galvanized metal buckets filled with water, floating candles and apples in them. Around the buckets we placed gourds, small pumpkins, leaves, acorns and more apples. We ordered the galvanized metal buckets from a horse supply website, bought the apples, pumpkins, and gourds from a local apple orchard, and had kids in the neighborhood collect acorns and pretty leaves. Also, to avoid expensive imported flowers for the church, we bought huge potted mums for $3 each from a local farmer." — *Tara*

These escort cards are on recycled hemp paper. The drift wood was found at a local lake. Holes were drilled into the wood to hold small vases and single flowers. This simple, yet stunning backdrop required few cut flowers.

spices or organic herbs needed along with the recipe. You could put the herbs in small gift tins, available by mail order or in local craft stores. Your guests will be reminded of your wedding day every time they cook with your thoughtful favor.

Eco-couple Send-offs

Traditionally, guests have tossed rice over newlyweds to wish them well as they exit the ceremony. Many churches and other ceremony sites have banned this practice, since rice can be slippery and potentially harmful to birds. Tossing birdseed can be dusty and your guests may inadvertently be spreading weeds. One alternative is to use biodegradable "ecofetti" from Ecoparti.com <www.ecoparti.com>, which comes in cute shapes that dissolve in water. Or consider having your guests toss "petal-fetti", a mix of herbs and petals available from Wedding Petals <www.weddingpetals.com>. Organic lavender buds are another option, which are about the size and shape of rice, lending a fragrant accent to the bridal path.

One thing we don't think should be flying over your heads is a cluster of butterflies. A swirl of butterflies lifting gracefully into the air to the delight of your guests sounds lovely; but the North American Butterfly Association <www.naba.org> explains that there are several serious hazards to wedding-related butterfly releases. They sum up this questionable activity by pointing out, "There's no need to release butterflies, they're already free." If you're still unconvinced and craving a monarch memory for your big day, at least read NABA's position before making your final decision.

WOW — Why Organic Weddings?

In Latin America, flowers are routinely sprayed with a pesticide cocktail of toxins and carcinogens — up to 650 gallons of chemicals per acre, per week. In total, conventional flower cultivation consumes more pesticides than any other agricultural sector. The majority of cut flowers sold in the US come from Latin American greenhouses, with more than 50 percent from Colombia. An estimated 20 percent of the pesticides used in Colombia on flower farms were banned or unregistered in the UK or the US.

(Sources: Institute for Global Communications (IGC) and Organic Bouquet <www.organicbouquet.com>.)

GREEN GIFTS TO GIVE AND GET

From this day forward, you can do more with any purchase you make from many major online stores simply by shopping through these gateway sites: Shop For Change <www.shopforchange.com> and iGive.com <www.igive.com>. Both sites are affiliated with brand-name merchants including amazon.com, Lands' End, Patagonia and Gaiam. On iGive.com, purchasers can even register their own cause-related organization for help with fundraising. At Shop For Change, purchases at their affiliated merchants result in donations of up to five percent to "non-profit groups working for peace, equality, human rights, education, and a cleaner environment."

A Favor for You

How about some great alternatives to the typical, mostly-empty, waste-of-paper wedding guest book, which sooner or later ends up in a box in the attic? Instead, collect your guests' signatures on a keepsake matboard that you can frame and display in your home. Any framing shop will be able to cut a piece of mat to fit either a standard frame like 16x20" or a custom size. Have them cut an inside space to fit a 5x7" photo of yourselves or one of your wedding invitations. Your guests can then sign the matboard during your wedding, creating a piece of art you will cherish long after your wedding day. Visit <www.organicweddings.com> for a similar idea, our Guest Sign-In Panels. Or, set out a bowl at your reception filled with small blank squares or strips of tree-free/recycled paper, each tied with a small loop of colorful ribbon, raffia or hemp yarn. Your wedding guests can write a short message or good wish and hang it on the branches of a "tree," which can be a live ornamental plant or some dry, twiggy branches. Even very young guests can write their names or draw you a picture. Your guests will have fun taking part in this project, and you'll end up with a beautiful collection of special messages from your friends and family that can later be incorporated into a scrapbook. A variation on this idea: use long strips of paper that can be folded and tied directly onto the branches, or furnish wide satin ribbon and fine-point fabric markers and tie the wishes right onto the tree.

Natural Nuptials

KATHERINE AND JOE — MAY 4
NEW YORK, NEW YORK

*K*atherine and Joe went on their first date while at college together in Ohio — but their second date wasn't until nine years later after reconnecting when a mutual friend brought Katherine to Joe's 30th birthday party in New York City. Their relationship grew, and two years later, Joe proposed to Katherine on her birthday.

"Joe proposed with a Burmese star ruby that I now wear in a necklace. The stone was a perfect match for me and I appreciated that he was daring enough to break away from the standard diamond," said Katherine. "Later on, I got the best

of both worlds when my aunt handed down my grandmother's diamond engagement ring to me."

The couple planned a wedding that was personal and unique to them. They chose Fort Tyron Park in Upper Manhattan, which is also the home of the Cloisters Museum, as the venue for their ceremony and reception. There was a great deal of meaning behind their choice; the park was a part of the groom's childhood and is just a five-minute walk from their current residence. Additionally, profits from their reception went to an organization dedicated towards restoration and maintenance of New York City parks.

"We held the reception at the park's New Leaf Café — a unique, for-profit establishment that's run by a non-profit group, the New York Restoration Project. So, ultimately our wedding will help support the park," said Joe. "Since I grew up in the neighborhood —and played in the park with our best man as a child — I remember when the old stone building was a poorly 🖝

Natural Nuptials

maintained snack bar. Now it's been restored and I have a great sense of local pride."

The ceremony was on one of the park's lawns overlooking the Hudson River, with the Palisades in the background. A rabbi who is a close friend of the groom performed the ceremony. With a nod to the bride's Scottish ancestry, two bagpipers provided the ceremony music. For her wedding dress, Katherine had a classic princess style gown custom-designed for her in natural hemp/silk fabric, with a coordinating silk eyelet shawl.

The luncheon reception for 75 guests included an organic mixed greens salad and other delicious dishes made with locally sourced ingredients from the Hudson River Valley area. For the reception music, the couple found a classical guitarist whose acoustic style provided just the right level of festivity at the event.

For wedding flowers, Katherine's well-intentioned plans for forcing her own organic crocus bulbs didn't work out quite as expected. So, she hired her design student neighbor to make natural-looking centerpieces. By avoiding

conventional roses altogether and buying what was most local at the NYC wholesale flower district, Katherine found a compromise that would work. "I didn't want to use roses, since I've read some harrowing articles about the pesticides and fungicides used in their cultivation," said Katherine.

Their honeymoon took them to the Scottish Hebrides where they did some camping and took some spectacular hikes through all sorts of terrain. "It was a nice break from the pre-packaged honeymoon and also a chance for me to learn more about my Scottish heritage," said Katherine.

Now enjoying life together as newlyweds, Katherine and Joe continue to have a connection to their wedding day through their community-supported agriculture (CSA) program. The couple picks up their organic, locally grown vegetables every week at the New Leaf Café, which is hosting their CSA's pick-up point. "It was satisfying — not to mention convenient — to celebrate our wedding locally and it's nice to have a continued connection to our reception site," said Joe.

Wedding Party Gift Ideas

They've been there for you, including helping you through your wedding plans. Now, they are sharing this important milestone in your life and you'd like to say thanks. Choose a gift that shows you care about them and the environment. In addition to the ideas here, find eco-gift ideas online in our Resources Directory <www.organicweddings.com/resources>.

For the Ladies: Consider making beautiful barrettes or headbands using vintage mother-of-pearl buttons, beads, or seashells, hand-selected by you. These items, as well as small pieces of vintage jewelry, can usually be found in local antique shops or flea markets. Personalize these gifts by presenting them on small recycled or eco-fiber cards. Or consider Eco-artware.com's unique perfume bottles and picture frames from recycled materials. Antique picture frames also make beautiful gifts. Encourage the important ladies in your life to pamper themselves naturally, with gifts of organic body care items from companies like Benedetta <www.benedetta.com> and Chestnut & Bay <www.chestnutand-bay.com>. Fair trade pashmina shawls, like those from Sunrise Pashmina <www.sunrise-pashmina.com>, do double duty as bridal party attire and lovely gifts.

For the Gentlemen: Consider giving antique or vintage cufflinks to wear at your wedding. Most tux and dress shirts are available with French cuffs, making cufflinks a special wedding memento. If your event is too casual for cufflinks, consider buying your groomsmen something eco-friendly that suits your event style or their personalities better. As with the ladies' shawls, you can give the men ties which will function both as part of their wedding outfits and as their thank-you gift. Vineyard Vines <www.vineyardvines.com> has a collection of beautiful silk tie patterns called "Tied to a Cause," from which a portion of the

"*I* always liked the convenience of special amenity baskets in the bathrooms at wedding receptions. For my wedding, I borrowed baskets from a recently married cousin and filled them with environmentally friendly products like a mini Tom's of Maine toothpaste, organic cotton personal products, natural breath mints and Burt's Bees lotion. I spent a little more money, but I liked the idea of introducing my friends and family to products that work great and are earth-friendly."

— *Gabrielle*

These eco-aware cufflinks were made using old typewriter keys. The groom gave each of his men a pair in their initials.

Words of Wisdom

AN INTERVIEW WITH DAVE SMITH, CO-FOUNDER AND PRESIDENT, ORGANIC BOUQUET

*D*ave Smith's dedication to organic living began when he worked as an executive assistant to Cesar Chavez, the founder of the first successful farm workers' union in US history. Inspired by a commitment to improving conditions for farm workers, Dave later went on to co-found Briarpatch Natural Foods Co-op and Smith & Hawken. He has been an executive and a director of Real Goods, Diamond Organics and Seeds of Change. In 2001, he co-founded Organic Bouquet, the first national organic floral company. He is a board member of the Ukiah Natural Foods Co-op and co-founder of the Mendocino Organic Network, an alliance of farmers and consumers promoting local, organic and sustainable farming.

Organic Weddings: Who or what shaped your life with respect to the values we see in your company and career?

Dave Smith: The four-year period I spent with Cesar Chavez and the Farmworkers Union was the defining experience of my life. Their commitment to non-violence was especially appealing and motivating. During that time, I learned how pesticide practices on large farms resulted in an enormous amount of harm being done to our environment, our personal health and the health of farmers, farmworkers and farmworkers' children. For example, I know of a farmworker who picked grapes in the fields during her pregnancy and then had a child with severe birth defects. This story and many others like it happen wherever farm workers are not protected against chemical toxins. However, for most consumers, out of sight is out of mind, and the suffering that goes on is invisible and unacknowledged. Yet this suffering is completely unnecessary. Organic farmers show us that every day. The negative impact of unsustainable farming methods is enormous, both socially and environmentally. I believe that the true heroes of our culture are the organic and biodynamic farmers who care enough to feed us with health from their vegetables and beauty from their flowers without chemical poisons. I enjoy being able to help support their hard work. ☞

Words of Wisdom (contd.)

☞ These experiences inspired me to co-found a natural foods co-op to increase access to healthy, organic foods. Later, I wanted to help support organic farmers and gardeners by importing superior hand-tools from England, which is how Smith & Hawken started. More recently, I co-founded a group in Northern California to promote local organic agriculture.

OW: Flowers are typically a focal point for many weddings, but have been largely overlooked when it comes to balancing ecology with style and tradition. Why might couples carefully consider their choices about wedding flowers?

DS: We need to take steps beyond buying organic food for our health and consider the health of the Earth, as well as the people toiling in the fields. Cultivated flowers are an area where it is less obvious what is going on behind the scenes in developing countries where most are grown. However, the use of pesticides and fumigants is rampant, causing untold damage to the water, air and soil in those countries. Equally disturbing are the health problems experienced by the workers, especially women and children. Flowers make a nice addition to embellishing a wedding, but as people learn more about the true journey from soil to bouquet, I hope more brides and grooms will think more about what is going on. Purchasing things like organic cotton clothing and organic flowers are steps that consider others, not just ourselves.

OW: What is something you do in your own home to reduce your ecological footprint?

DS: We recycle all of our paper, bags, plastic, bottles, and cans. My family has been purchasing organic food almost exclusively for over 30 years, and we also compost our food wastes and the manure from our two horses. We use the rich soil to fertilize our garden. By the way, people who also have compost piles should be aware to never put store-bought, non-organic flowers in their compost because they are contaminated with several pesticides.

OW: Why organic weddings?

DS: What a great way to start a marriage! We are all connected with each other and with the environment, and making that statement in front of friends and family by purchasing, providing and displaying organics shows a fundamental, heartfelt commitment beyond your own immediate cares and concerns. . ❦

sale price is donated to non-profit organizations like the Breast Cancer Alliance and the September 11th Children's Fund. If golf is in your plans, hand out biodegradable corn-based golf tees. Eco Golf <www.ecogolf.com> offers personalized tees, as well as golf balls that dissolve with water over time — both good ideas considering the billions of tees and golf balls that are lost outdoors every year. How about giving the gift of time? With Citizen's fashionable Eco-Drive solar-powered watches, you can.

For the Kids: Celebrate your smallest wedding party attendants with gifts that are age-appropriate, fun, eco-friendly and made to last. Childsake <www.childsake.com> offers a variety of children's gifts that deal with themes of nature and the environment. Many are made with natural materials from environmentally responsible sources. The company also donates five percent of profits to non-profit organizations that work to improve the lives of children and better the environment.

Eco-gifts to Get: Remarkable Registries

While registering for gifts is not a must-do, most guests find it helpful in decreasing the angst of finding the perfect wedding gift. However, think seriously about where you register for your gifts. The buying power represented by wedding gift registries is another great opportunity to put more dollars to work for your environmental and social values. Your guests' generosity can be multiplied when you sign up for gift options that benefit society and the planet.

"*I* love handmade pottery and really wanted my everyday dishes to be handmade by a local potter, not mass-produced for a department store. I looked on the Web and visited a handful whose work I really liked. We chose a husband and wife team from Maine and they already had a registry system in place. It was not Web-based, but my mom coordinated the effort to get her side of my family to buy the items and we ended up with 12 place settings of handmade pottery." — *Jennifer*

Eco-friendly registry: Through the Organic Weddings website <www.organicweddings.com/shop/>, you can select from a wide array of stylish, earth-friendly items for your home. We have collected the finest bedroom, bath and kitchen items, from 100 percent organic cotton sheets to recycled glassware. You'll find everything you'll need to help you

create a healthy home that will keep you both relaxed and energized long after your wedding is over. However, even if you choose to set up a department store bridal registry, you can still do your best to make it green. Avoid conventionally grown cotton, items that are likely to get thrown out, and household goods that might have been sewn by sweatshop labor. This information won't be readily available at department stores, but you can still do your best to ask questions or make a note of where items are produced. Whenever possible, choose products made with natural materials that you know to be less damaging to the environment.

Charitable Giving Registry: Through the I Do Foundation <www.idofoundation.org> you can select a non-profit organization to benefit from donations made by your guests. Guests simply locate your registry on the website and make a donation in your name. This is also a great option for people who don't wish to receive any gifts. Sometimes, telling guests "no gifts" may confuse well-wishers who really want to give a gift in celebration of your day. Instead, let it be known (through the grapevine) that you would find heartfelt meaning in their donation to one of your favorite philanthropies in place of a material item. If you don't already have an organization in mind, consider one that is approved by the American Institute of Philanthropy <www.charitywatch.org>, or by the Better Business Bureau's Wise Giving Alliance <www.give.org>.

The I Do Foundation also makes it possible to use the conventional gift registry system to benefit charitable organizations. They have teamed with

> "*We* decided to have three gift registries, not only to be able to register for a wide range of items, but more importantly so that we could help support two local businesses and an Internet-based registry which specialized in eco-friendly products for the home."
>
> — *Kathy*

DON'T TAKE THE WRAP

Because recycled wrapping paper can be difficult to find, eco-gift givers (and receivers) prefer to skip conventional gift-wrap. Get creative by reusing handled gift bags and decorating the outside. One of our favorite ideas is to ask your guests to wrap their gifts in fabric. After you unwrap all your gifts, you'll have great fun piecing the fabric together to make anything from tablecloths to drapes to quilts. You'll be amused for years trying to remember which guests gave what gifts in which fabric.

retailers such as Target and Cooking.com, who will donate between three and eight percent of the amount purchased to carefully selected non-profit organizations. There is no additional cost to your guests; all they have to do is make their purchases through your registry on the I Do Foundation's website. You can even use your honeymoon to raise money for charity. Make your plans through the I Do Foundation's travel sponsor and five percent of the package price will be donated to a non-profit organization.

Maybe you'd like to ask for the gift of time? Get your guests to give of their time by encouraging them to find a volunteering opportunity in their local area. VolunteerMatch <www.volunteermatch.org> is a non-profit, online

Photography Fundamentals

Your wedding photos will become cherished keepsakes. However, conventional photography uses many chemicals, paper and plastic film. Digital photography is emerging as a high-quality and more environmentally friendly method of photo capture and production. Digital photography also allows the photographer to preview the photos during the event and re-shoot if the exposure or other elements could be improved. Wedding photographer Erika Sidor (whose work is featured in this book) loves working with her professional digital camera: "It is fast and accurate, and it provides me with the results I demand," she says. When shooting a wedding digitally, Erika has the freedom to shoot more photos because there is no expensive film and no time-consuming rewinding and reloading required. Instead of stacks of proofs and negatives, the entire collection of images can be downloaded onto a CD for the bride and groom to review. Rather than getting thrown away, the undesirable photos are simply deleted. Whether or not you choose digital photography, one thing you can do to reduce your photo impact is to avoid purchasing disposable cameras for each table. The environmental and dollar cost of doing this isn't worth the mostly poor quality photos many couples get back. If you're looking for candids your photographer might not catch, encourage friends and family to bring their own cameras and share their (much better) photos with you.

service that helps interested volunteers get involved with community service organizations throughout the US. Find other creative ideas at Married For Good <www.MarriedForGood.com>.

CHAPTER 8

Honeymoon and Wedding Travel

IT'S EASY TO BE GREEN with your honeymoon and other wedding travel plans. Transportation is a major environmental impact area, so your conscious choices really do make a difference. When determining event logistics, consider how you can lessen the environmental impacts of your friends' and family's travels. Once the wedding celebration is over, you'll look forward to some quality time together. Whether you decide to hike the Appalachian Trail or make a conventional trip more earth-friendly, honeymoons large and small can be planned in ways that reflect your sense of environmental and social responsibility.

PLANES, TRAINS AND AUTOMOBILES

Your invitations are in the mail and before too long, your nuptials will inspire countless travel plans. In our global society, an invitation to a wedding is often

Destroying rainforest for economic gain is like burning a Renaissance painting to cook a meal.
— Edward O. Wilson

an invitation to travel hundreds, if not thousands of miles in order to take part in the celebration. The environmental impacts from travel come primarily from the fuel used by planes, trains and automobiles, as well as their associated emissions. If you're planning to hold your celebration in a destination outside your local area, encourage people to carpool to the ceremony and reception. This will also ease parking and traffic hassles.

More Trees, Please!

If you have a lot of friends and family flying in from different states or even different countries, you might think about a sponsoring a tree-planting program to balance out the carbon dioxide that's released to the environment through air travel. There are a few tree-planting organizations that will do the guesswork and the legwork for you:

This bride finds an eco-friendly means of travel to the ceremony with a little help from her dad. The gown is a bateau neck design in hemp/silk.

Trees for the Future: Trees for the Future's Trees for Travel program <www.treesftf.org/travel.htm> plants trees in developing countries to offset the carbon dioxide created by your honeymoon and/or guest travel. For every dollar you (or your guests) donate to the program, Trees for the Future will plant 10 carbon dioxide-absorbing trees in your name. For a minimum donation of $30 they'll send you a certificate showing the number of trees that have been planted on your behalf. Maybe you'll decide to estimate the total miles that guests will be traveling to your wedding and sponsor enough trees to offset the carbon output. You could let your guests know by including a note about the program when you send out save-the-date notices. Or tell your guests about Trees for Travel and encourage them to sign up when they buy their plane tickets. Another idea is to ask for a tree-planting certificate as a wedding gift.

MarryMe Woods: MarryMe Woods is a project of Future Forests <www.futureforests.com>, which plants trees in selected woods in the UK. You can purchase a package of two trees, which comes with a certificate and a map showing the location of your trees. Or, you can designate a spot in the woods where your guests' trees will be planted all together, creating a living legacy to commemorate your special, carbon-neutral day.

Heifer Project International: Heifer Project International <www.heifer.org> runs programs to provide cows, goats, and yes, trees to communities in developing countries. You can buy saplings online for between $10 and $60, which are given in your name to families who will benefit from the fast-growing trees that provide food, windbreaks, fencing, better soil and more.

Travel Cool: An innovative program of the Better World Club (see page 116), Travel Cool also lets you reduce greenhouse gas emissions every time you book a flight or rental car. With your tax-deductible donation of $11 per round-

THE NATIONAL PARK SYSTEM

The US National Park System <www.nps.gov> receives over 265 million visits each year — more than National Football League attendance, Disney attractions and Universal Studios attractions combined — according to Xanterra, a parks management company. From spectacular scenery to outdoor recreation, any of these 379 natural treasures could be the perfect place to explore and relax together on your honeymoon.

trip domestic flight, Travel Cool will invest in energy-saving projects and technologies to fight global warming, such as replacing outdated oil-burning boilers in public schools.

A Better Way than AAA

If you're one of the 45 million members of the American Automobile Association (AAA), it may shock you to learn that along with providing travel planning and roadside assistance, AAA has lobbied Congress to fight the Clean Air Act, defeat fuel economy standards, and oppose measures for better public transportation. Aligned with automakers and other industry lobbyists, AAA has thrown the weight of its enormous membership behind these anti-environment efforts. Most eco-minded motorists have no idea their membership dues go to support this kind of advocacy. What can you do? AAA members can speak up by writing to the club in support of the environment. But if you're fed up enough to quit, check out the alternative — the Better World Club <www.betterworldclub.com> is a roadside assistance and travel club that "strives to balance your transportation needs with your desire to protect the environment." One percent of their revenues go towards environmental cleanup efforts worldwide. Every effort to drive less is important, but ours is hardly a car-free society. The Better World Club can get you a deal on auto insurance, help you find a green hotel or a hybrid/electric rental car, or give you a hand planning environmentally-conscious vacations. They also feature the nation's first bicycle roadside assistance program, along with all the standard auto services such as flat tire and lockout assistance. Knowing the damage that car travel does to our environment, many people are signing up with this innovative and responsible organization.

MAPPING THE WAY TO A GREENER FUTURE

Eco-tourism isn't just for tropical resorts. Even if your honeymoon destination is the bright lights of a big city, you can still be an eco-traveler. From Bangkok to Berkeley to Barcelona, and in more than 200 cities and regions around the world, you can pick up a Green Map <www.greenmap.org> to direct you to parks, bike paths, natural food stores and more. Each map is a local, independent effort, but all are united by a common set of symbols, coordinated by the New York-based Green Map System. They're great for business travel, too.

Alternative-Fueled Vehicles

Through Budget Rent-a-Car, EV Rental <www.evrental.com> offers electric and natural gas powered vehicles at 12 locations in California, Arizona, Pennsylvania and Washington, DC — the first time alternative fuel vehicles have been available to rent in the US. Renters are given a list of recharging locations at nearby business, entertainment and tourist spots. You can find more on their website or by calling Budget at 877-EV-RENTAL. Remember, the more people ask about alternative vehicles, the sooner we'll see them as a standard option at rental car counters. So, the next time you book a rental, be sure to inquire about the hybrid, electric, natural gas, or just high fuel economy options. If you are having (or attending) an event in or near Boston, Washington, DC, San Francisco or Denver, consider the services of Zip Car <www.zipcar.com>. This company is revolutionizing the car-sharing concept with its rental fleet of trendy and fuel-efficient cars.

UNDERSTANDING ECO-TOURISM

The International Ecotourism Society defines ecotourism as "responsible travel to natural areas that conserves the environment and sustains the well-being of local people." It means low-impact travel, minimizing the use of non-renewable resources as well as conserving water and energy and reducing waste. There are growing numbers of eco-resorts and eco-tour services that cater to travelers who care strongly about the environment and tourism's effect on local people and cultures. Ecotourism also promotes biodiversity conservation and strengthens the local economy of the travel destination. Local businesses such as inns and guide services can thrive when tourists spend their dollars in the area, rather than staying at large resorts owned by multinational chains. Sustainable tourism can give people economic options, when they might otherwise resort to selling off sensitive natural products such as coral or furs from endangered species.

Ecotourism is an approach to travel that aims for meaningful cross-cultural experiences between the traveler and host. Eco-travel options cover a wide range, from trekking adventures that highlight local biology to relaxing vacations on the beach. What these tour and lodge operators have in common is an understanding that tourist destinations can suffer from their own popularity. Eco-tourists make positive choices by carefully considering the impact they have on natural places.

" *We* went to Bedarra Island, an eco-resort off the northwest coast of Australia. We didn't stay at the resort (it was full) but we rented a house complete with solar power and a rainwater collection tank, on the very private other side of the island. This seemed better than the resort because we could do everything at our own pace and we love to cook our own food. We needed a boat to get to the house, where we were dropped off with our food for a week. We had a selection of seafood, champagne, fresh fruits and vegetables, etc., all of which my husband had pre-ordered. We just hung out on the beach, napped, snorkeled and read. Our biggest activity was kayaking around the island while watching the reef sharks and beautiful fish swimming below. It was absolutely unbelievable. The water was turquoise, clear, and the same temperature as a warm bath." — *Elise*

Besides great photographs, they also come home with broader horizons and a richer global perspective. A good place to start for both information and practical links to lodge and tour operators is the International Ecotourism Society's site <www.ecotourism.org>. You can search by region or specific country for everything from cruises to educational tours. Planeta.com <www.planeta.com> is also a comprehensive site worth visiting to learn more about ecotourism around the world.

Trampled by Travel

In most all-inclusive package tours, more than 80 percent of travelers' fees go to the airlines, hotels and other international companies, not to local businesses or workers. Resorts and hotels often over-consume natural resources like water

Do-Gooder Honeymoons

If you and your honey share a passion for helping others, why not spend your first vacation as a married couple on a volunteer trip? Whether building homes in rural America or counting butterflies in Thailand, volunteering on your vacation can help the people and places you visit as well as offering a fun and rewarding getaway.

A number of established, reputable organizations offer cross-cultural tours that provide opportunities for service as well as educational exchange. Trips vary in length from 1 to 12 weeks, and volunteers usually pay a fee for the program. Unlike conventional vacations or eco-tourism, volunteer trips offer a structured way to come in direct contact with people from the host country. It involves hard work, but you'll enjoy a rewarding trip and meet more real people than the average tourist. Here are some suggestions:

• Habitat for Humanity International's Global Village trips <www.habitat.org/GV>, where volunteers work alongside members of the host community to build homes and raise awareness of affordable housing issues. Trips range from 7-15 days in length and cost between $1,200-$3,800. It's not all work and no play, though — team members usually balance building days with three to five days of R&R. Trips within the US are also available. ☞

and power, forcing utility prices up and causing blackouts and water shortages for locals. According to the International Ecotourism Society, many negative environmental and social impacts result from today's travel practices. For example, in popular resort areas like Cancun and Hawaii, overbuilt beachfront hotels have contributed to beach erosion,

WOW — WHY ORGANIC WEDDINGS?

One round-trip between New York and Los Angeles creates about one ton of carbon dioxide per passenger — 400 tons or more for a typical, fully loaded Boeing 737 aircraft. Offset all those greenhouse gases by planting trees. One tree can absorb 50 pounds of carbon dioxide every year — about one ton of carbon dioxide over an estimated 40-year lifespan.

flooding and the disappearance of natural wetlands, and generate mountains of garbage without adequate means of disposal. In Nepal, the rapid growth of the

Do-Gooder Honeymoons

- Earthwatch Institute's <www.earthwatch.org> volunteer expeditions, which have been involving members of the public in scientific field research since 1972. Held in 45 countries, trips last between 10-14 days and cost $1,500-$2,000 on average. Choose from trips focused on biodiversity conservation, aquatic ecosystems, global health, and more. No special scientific skills are required in order to help the lead scientists collect data.

- Cross-Cultural Solutions <www.crosscultural-solutions.org> fosters cultural exchange and understanding through its volunteer programs in Brazil, China, Costa Rica, Ghana, India, Peru, Russia, Thailand, and Tanzania. Participants work alongside local people on sustainable community initiatives that are designed and driven locally. By working together, volunteers gain a unique perspective on the host culture and environment. Trips last between 2-12 weeks and fees start at $1,985, which is tax-deductible for US residents.

- The American Hiking Society <www.american-hiking.org> offers over 70 one- and two-week camping trips through US National Forests, National Parks, and State Parks. Volunteers maintain and build trails, cabins, and shelters while exploring the backcountry wilderness. Trips cost only $80 and yes, there are national parks in Hawaii.

"*We* spent our honeymoon at the same place we were married — on the beautiful islands of Captiva and Sanibel, Florida. The two islands have very strict building and zoning laws so they are developed in an ecologically friendly way; no high rises; no removal of native trees, no asphalt driveways, etc. Forty-five percent of Sanibel is protected land, so there is plenty of open space and trails. We enjoyed kayaking, snorkeling, biking, swimming and fishing — all without the stress of traveling anywhere new — it was a great way to keep celebrating." — *Ally*

CAN WE TALK?

As much as possible, you should consider whether suppliers of travel services and products comply with pollution control practices, health and safety measures as well as labor standards wherever they operate. Talk to your travel agent, or if you are making your own arrangements, don't be afraid to inquire directly.

trekking industry has increased pollution in Kathmandu and caused dangerous crowding and destruction of trails. Logging for hotel building materials and cooking fires has led to deforestation, flooding and landslides as far away as Bangladesh. In Yellowstone National Park, trash left by tourists has led to forced relocation of bears and their untimely deaths.

IMPROVING CONVENTIONAL TRAVEL

Tourism is the world's largest and fastest growing industry. According to recent statistics, tourism provides 10 percent of the world's income and employs almost one-tenth of the world's workforce. By the year 2010, these numbers will double. While eco-travel is a great way to go, most travel today is through established networks of conventional services and accommodations. According to Green Seal, the average hotel purchases more products in one week than 100 families do in a year. Because of this, the greening of mainstream travel is an enormous opportunity to conserve resources and increase awareness of environmental impacts from the hospitality industry. A growing number of hotels are doing their part for Mother Nature. Depending on the size of your wedding, your guests may collectively be spending thousands of dollars on lodging in the area of your event. This represents a huge opportunity for you to support green hotels.

Going for the Green

The hospitality industry has yet to come up with a gold standard for green lodging; as of now there aren't any independent certifications that are as recognizable as the USDA standards for organic food. However, the websites listed here can help you and your guests identify a wide range of lodging facilities around the world, that are committed to saving water and energy, reducing solid waste, and purchasing products such as non-toxic cleaning supplies and post-consumer recycled paper. Some of the creative things they are doing include using healthy alternatives to chlorine in pools, using solar energy to light signs and walkways, and replacing water intensive lawns with drought-resistant native landscaping.

- The Greener Lodging Directory
  <www.greenerlodging.com>
- Co-Op America's National Green Pages <www.greenpages.org>
- The Green Hotels Association <www.greenhotels.com>
- Green Seal's Environmental Lodging Standards
  <www.greenseal.org/standards/lodgingproperties.htm>
- Green Globe 21 <www.greenglobe21.com>, established by the World Travel and Tourism Council
- Travel Organic <www.travelorganic.com>

Many hotels are making large strides in environmental progress. A pioneer in the field, Saunders Hotel Group, created SHINE (Saunders Hotels Initiatives

WOW — WHY ORGANIC WEDDINGS?

Any idea how much money is spent per year on honeymoon travel? Nearly $5 billion. Now imagine if half of all honeymoons involved some amount of ecotourism or eco-consciousness, for instance including a stay at a green hotel. That would provide a big boost for environmentally responsible businesses and the trickle down effect would be enormous.

ECO-HOTELS 101

- Avoid disposables for food and beverage service.
- Install energy-saving compact fluorescent lighting and water-saving devices.
- Encourage in-room recycling, less frequent linen changes and refillable bathroom amenities like shampoo.
- Offer organic, local and sustainable menus; reduce food waste and compost scraps.
- Buy recycled paper products with high post-consumer waste content.
- Sponsor nature tours and other educational activities celebrating the local flora and fauna.

Natural Nuptials

LIZA AND STEFAN — FEBRUARY 16
OLD SAN JUAN, PUERTO RICO

Liza and Stefan, having cultural roots from around the world, planned a spectacular wedding that celebrated their local and international connections. The weekend of activities was set for the bride's hometown in Puerto Rico. An antique Spanish historical building belonging to

a nonprofit cultural organization was chosen for both the ceremony and reception. This unique location helped to minimize transportation needs for the 170 guests and provided a picturesque backdrop to their elegant evening.

The couple, both having worked for non-profit organizations, sought to make a positive impact with their celebration. "Stefan and I saw our wedding as an opportunity to share with others what we believe in, who we are, and to celebrate those things with our friends and family," said Liza. Through their wedding-related purchases, they supported small, independent businesses and artisans. They also registered for wedding gifts at Ten Thousand Villages, a store known for its fair trade handicrafts from around the world.

Because of their concerns for the environment, Liza and Stefan chose tree-free and recycled papers for their intricate wedding invitations and ceremony programs. Both were in multiple languages, emphasizing their international heritage, and included the native Puerto Rican Taino petroglyph symbol of a coqui, a tiny tree frog, along with the Taino word "areyto" for celebration. A calligrapher created their ketubah, a Jewish wedding certificate, in five languages: English, Hebrew, Spanish, German and Armenian.

Natural Nuptials

☞ The couple wrote the English text themselves and had friends fluent in each of the other languages provide translations.

Special touches were woven throughout the wedding to help guests appreciate the culture and natural beauty of Puerto Rico. Tables had names of local trees, bird, flowers, fruits, and animals. Potted orchids graced the tables and were later given away as special gifts. The flower girl and ring bearer wore folkloric outfits complete with red sashes sewn by the bride's aunt. The flower girl wore a local flower in her hair and the ring bearer wore a "pava," a typical Puerto Rican straw hat. "For us, spending time with family and friends while enjoying Puerto Rico was a priority, so we filled the days before and after with activities like a beach trip, a museum trip and a trip to the mountains." Stefan said.

As well as forgoing an engagement ring, the couple chose wedding bands that provided special meaning; one had belonged to Stefan's mother, and the other was made by a jeweler in the family. "I felt strongly that I didn't want Stefan to buy me a diamond engagement ring. Stefan and I both felt that it was an example of a corporate ad campaign selling people their dreams, not to mention the long history of exploitation, brutality, and environmental impacts connected to diamond mining," said Liza.

The couple valued the community of friends and family that formed throughout the wedding weekend. "As people helped us out rehearsing music, tying bows on programs, and wrapping presents, they got to know one another — quirks, talents, and all. They all made a wonderful contribution to our wedding. Each element was special for the love, care, jokes, sweat and tears put into it," said Liza.

The newlyweds brought their international point of view with them on their five-month honeymoon trek around the world. They traveled to 12 countries, including Kenya, Ethiopia, Egypt, Israel, Germany and Armenia. They intentionally kept their travels close to local communities to experience and learn as much as possible, which has broadened their perspectives on making a positive difference in people's lives, as they both embark upon careers in medicine. 🐾

to Nurture the Environment) at their environmental award-winning Boston properties: The Lenox and Copley Square Hotels, and the Comfort Inn & Suites near Logan Airport. With 90 initiatives including state-of-the-art ozone laundries and energy management systems, the S.H.I.N.E. program annually saves 1,700,000 gallons of drinking water, eliminates 37 tons of trash, conserves 110,000 kilowatt hours of electricity, and saves 175 trees through paper recycling. Another notable eco-hotel is the 193-room Sheraton Rittenhouse Square

Trolleys are a fun, eco-friendly way to help guests get from one location to another.

Hotel in Philadelphia, Pennsylvania. It has been renovated top to bottom with many environmental materials: recycled granite for flooring, recycled wood pallets for furniture, improved indoor air quality and even organic, natural and chemical-free alternatives for mattresses and bedding.

Smaller inns are doing their part, too. One notable example is the Brewery Gulch Inn of Mendocino, California, which was named one of the Ten Most Romantic Inns for 2002 (by American Historic Inns Guidebooks). The Brewery Gulch Inn is the only inn or hotel in California that is certified by the CCOF (California Certified Organic Farmers) for their organic products. The inn itself was built from carefully eco-salvaged redwood logs that had been lying at the bottom of the nearby Big River for over 100 years. From the Inn's compost systems to their acres of organic gardens, from their water efficient practices to their partnership with the local Audubon Society, this inn is another model for how every lodging facility, whether large or small, can go for the green.

Spreading the Word

Be aware that in many cases, you'll probably have to do some sleuthing to find out how eco-friendly an establishment really is. So if you want to know, be ready to ask the questions. When you call around to inquire about group rates for your guests, it's a perfect time to ask the sales person or manager a few environmental questions. For example, does the hotel offer the option to reuse sheets and towels instead of having them changed daily? Does the property have an efficient, energy management system in the guestrooms? Is there recycling in guest and function rooms, as well as behind the scenes? Do they use energy efficient lighting? Let the hotel know that their environmental performance is part of your decision criteria

on where you and your guests will stay. By asking a few questions, you'll be able to offer your guests a greener option when they're making their hotel reservations, as well as to encourage hotels to do more.

To get you started, the Council for Environmentally Responsible Economies (CERES) has created a Best Practice Survey as part of their pioneering Green Hotels Initiative. Their criteria include efforts toward envi-

Cruise Ship Blues

After months of wedding planning, doesn't a sun-soaked cruise vacation filled with leisurely days, fine dining and entertainment sound appealing? However, despite what the glitzy ads for cruise lines want you to believe, there are some serious reasons to think twice before choosing a cruise for your honeymoon. While it may be the fastest-growing segment of leisure travel, the cruise industry leaves behind plenty of nasty debris in its wake.

In his revealing book *Cruise Ship Blues*, sociologist and former cruise-goer Ross Klein exposes the darker side of cruising. From environmental to social considerations, the cruise industry could use a sustainability makeover. A typical cruise ship carries anywhere from 2,000 to 5,000 people and is essentially a mini-city, complete with shops, casinos, recreation facilities, photofinishers and more. On land, an operation of that size would have to answer to the EPA on standards like sewage treatment, but cruise ships

are exempt, most sailing under the flags of foreign nations. An average vessel generates 30,000 gallons a day of raw sewage, which can be dumped straight into the ocean as long as it's more than three miles off a US shore. Royal Caribbean International estimates that on a seven-day cruise, a ship will produce 141 gallons of photo chemicals, 7 gallons of dry-cleaning waste, 13 gallons of used paints, and 3 pounds of medical waste. Not to mention the 255,000 gallons per day of graywater, from showers, sinks, and laundry, carrying chemicals and detergents into the sea.

Over the years, cruise lines have been fined millions and millions of dollars for their illegal dumping, but these fines on the most egregious offenders have not led to any dramatic improvements in the industry's overall sense of responsibility. According to reports, Royal Caribbean was fined over $30 million from 1998-2000 for a myriad of environmental offenses, including oil and hazardous waste ☞

ronmentally-preferable practices and staff education. Use the survey to get ideas about other simple questions to ask about energy efficiency, environmental purchasing, water conservation, and more. Learn more about the initiative and check out the survey at <www.ceres.org/our_work/ghi.htm>.

Whenever you (or your friends and family) travel for business or pleasure, take along the Green Hotels Initiative's Guest Request Card. Printed cards can be

Cruise Ship Blues

☞ dumping and falsifying records. In 2002, Carnival Corporation was fined $18 million for illegal oil discharges. It is a sad irony that these companies don't take more of a leadership position in protecting the very waters and ports-of-call in beautiful surroundings that enable their businesses to flourish.

These floating resorts also have less than perfect records on customer-friendliness. However, beyond the disappointments of wily advertising and unmet expectations, cruises can be downright hazardous for passengers and on-board staff. The close quarters on cruise ships can harbor unwanted germs such as those that cause illnesses like the much-reported Norwalk virus. Regarding employees, cruise ships have been called "sweatshops at sea," regularly employing low-paid on-board staff who frequently work 80 hours a week for 10 or 12 months straight.

Service workers have little room to complain about wages and working conditions because many ships are registered in countries such as Panama and Liberia. As a result, they are functionally exempt from widely accepted and enforced labor standards, environmental regulations and tax codes.

Not all is lost; you still can take that cruise of your eco-dreams if you do your homework and ask questions. Take a look at Ross Klein's website <www.cruisejunkie.com> for updated information on cruise industry developments regarding labor, the environment, ship safety and security. Search out respected organizations like World Wildlife Fund and National Geographic, which offer smaller-scale but sustainable and nature-oriented cruises. These types of eco-cruises won't give you that "floating city" feeling, but by redirecting your travel dollars toward more mindful operators, you'll be sending a message that *all* cruises should have a conscience. 🐾

ordered from CERES' web site or a printable version can be downloaded at: <
www.ceres.org/our_work/ghi/guest_request_sample.pdf. Let hotel management
know your preferences for waste-minimizing and energy-reducing measures and
then give them feedback on how well they met your expectations. "Customer
comments, either written or verbal, are important to any lodging establishment,"
reports Tedd Saunders, executive vice president of Environmental Affairs for the
Saunders Hotel Group. Include a photocopy of the Check-In section when you
send out wedding invitations so your guests can help spread the word to hotel
managers about environmental impacts. Your requests will make a difference.

Above all, don't pass up the opportunity to use your honeymoon and wedding travel to raise your ecological consciousness. See our Resources Directory,
both online and in the back of this book, for many more great companies and
websites to help you plan the eco-friendly event of your dreams.

CHAPTER 9

Newlyweds and Natural Living

BEYOND YOUR WEDDING DAY is the opportunity for a lifetime full of natural living. A sustainable, satisfying lifestyle that balances ecology, style and tradition *every day* is right at your fingertips. While volumes have been written on the topics we present in this chapter, our goal here is to whet your appetite and frame your thinking on these important elements of living a good life. By setting up a natural home, getting involved with socially responsible investing, streamlining your consumption habits and choosing better food, you will be a catalyst for great changes.

LIFESTYLES OF THE SUSTAINABLE AND STYLISH

Sustainable living is reducing your ecological impact on the planet given the realities of our modern lifestyles. From junk mail to credit card debt, millions of

> "
> What's the use
> of a fine house
> if you haven't got
> a tolerable planet
> to put it on?
> — Henry David
> Thoreau
> "

Americans have mountains of clutter and stress, but not enough time, sense of security, or balance between life and work. Growing numbers share similar doubts about whether this manner of consumption is the secret to happiness.

WOW — WHY ORGANIC WEDDINGS?

The average New York City household discards two pounds of organic waste each day — adding up to more than one million tons of organic material a year. Even if you live in a city, composting your food scraps is easy. Learn more at <www.nycompost.org>.

As newlyweds with your nesting instinct in full swing, you're prone to feeling like you're on a "more stuff!" binge. What can help is finding ways to simplify and pay better attention to the waste and environmental toll that our spending habits leave behind, both globally and locally. Thus, in your journey to becoming a greener consumer, the first question to ask is whether you really need to make a purchase in the first place.

Don't get overwhelmed by all the possible changes. Instead, make steady steps in the right direction. Start small by replacing one product at a time with a more eco-friendly alternative as you use it up. Other changes are larger and may only be possible at certain times in your life, like minimizing your need to drive based on where you choose to live and work. Learn more about living a sustainable and stylish life from the Center for a New American Dream <www.newdream.org>, or pick up a copy of *The Better World Handbook,* by Ellis Jones et al., for an inspiring read.

Here are some tips to get you started:

- Reduce and reuse: Take care of what you already have and avoid buying more unless it's really needed. Buy used or "gently worn" items when possible.

- Recycle: Recycle your own trash and close the loop by buying items made from recycled or reused materials (especially post-consumer waste paper). For example, if you use paper towels — as 90% of American households do — buy 100% recycled. US consumers discard over 3,000 tons of paper towels every day, since they are unable to be recycled.

- Be transportation efficient: Walk, bicycle or take public transportation. The well-respected Union of Concerned Scientists states that the best thing you can do to reduce your ecological footprint is to reduce your car usage as much as possible. If you must have a car, avoid gas-guzzling SUVs and buy the most fuel-efficient, lowest polluting car you can afford. At home, choose Energy Star rated appliances and electrical items like computers. Buy compact fluorescent light bulbs. Minimize heating and cooling requirements from non-renewable resources. Avoid or minimize your use of high-impact items such as power-boats, gasoline-powered yard equipment and recreational off-road driving.

- Divert as much as possible from the waste stream: Avoid unnecessary packaging. Find ways to reuse, recycle, compost or give away. Your last resort should be the landfill.

- Consider social factors: Fair trade and fair labor practices are important in our global economy. Visit <www.responsibleshopper.org> and <www.fairtradefederation.org> to learn more.

A Thirsty Planet

NSF International <www.nsf.org> reports nearly 97 percent of the world's water is either salt or otherwise undrinkable. Another two percent is locked in ice caps and glaciers, leaving one percent for all of our fresh water needs. Every household needs to do their part to lessen their burden on our water supply. Simple steps include conservation through water-saving toilets, faucets and showerheads, as well as changing personal habits like turning off the faucet when brushing teeth. Always be vigilant about consumption, particularly in the summertime. Minimize water pressure when you turn on the faucet to wash up or rinse dishes or food. Reduce water use for gardens by collecting rainwater into recycled plastic water barrels. Pollutants are prevalent in many municipal and private water sources, so many people filter their water at home and work. Before choosing a water filter, check out its NSF rating <www.nsfconsumer.org> and learn more about water issues. Finally, be careful what you put down the drain and toilet. Water contaminants related to drugs, beauty product ingredients, and toxic cleaning products like chlorine bleach are not yet adequately filtered out.

Natural Nuptials

ELISE AND JOL — DECEMBER 28
DAYLESFORD, AUSTRALIA

While they had once been high school sweethearts in their native Australia, it wasn't until several years later when both were living in California that Elise and Jol reconnected as a couple. During one of their favorite forest hikes, Jol proposed at a serene spot in the shade of 2,000-year-old redwood trees.

Their mutual respect for the earth naturally became a guide for their wedding plans and helped them avoid elements that neither considered meaningful. "Most important to us was that our guests were able to celebrate, enjoy and relax with the simple pleasures of great people and great food in a natural setting," says Elise. They chose a working lavender farm — in full bloom on their wedding day — for their ceremony and reception. It set the tone for a celebration of natural beauty, showcasing simplicity and splendor while paring back on wasteful expenses.

Invitations highlighting the couple's plans for supporting the environment throughout the two-day celebration were printed on 100% post-consumer waste paper. Guests were encouraged to book accommodations together, as well as to reserve seats on a bus that would carry them to and from the reception. Elise and Jol arranged for a number of trees to be planted to offset the carbon dioxide produced by everyone's travel.

By simplifying wherever possible, Elise and Jol cut down on wedding stress. The ☞

Natural Nuptials

bridesmaids were free to choose their own dresses but remained within general color guidelines, so that their dresses and the groomsmen's attire complemented each other. One of Elise's sisters learned to do make-up and hair, which made getting ready "fun and relaxing." On the morning of the wedding, a private teacher led the bride's family in a calming yoga class. As a filmmaker, Elise was comfortable with coordinating all the details; however, family members took over at the end so she could just relax and enjoy the celebration.

Gathered outside under the trees, the guests encircled the couple at the ceremony and also sat in a circle at their candlelit reception, an arrangement that "kept the focus on the group rather than just on the bride and groom." Immediately following the ceremony, Elise and Jol spent fifteen minutes alone. "It gave us a chance to simply enjoy each other and the moment, before returning to the celebration," says Elise. The outdoor setting allowed Elise and Jol to forgo most decorations, instead using native greens, vines and fruits that had been harvested from local farms. Their caterer used all organic and local ingredients, and plans were made for leftover food to be given to a shelter. Food scraps were composted and other waste was recycled where possible. All dishes, cups and silverware at the reception were reusable and the gray dishwater (with non-toxic, biodegradable soap bubbles) went to watering plants on the farm.

Forgoing the standard guest book, the couple captured their guests' well wishes by preparing a board with the words Love, Nature, Community and Marriage written in calligraphy, around which guests wrote notes. Elise and Jol framed this expressive wedding memento and display it in their home to remind them of their celebration.

Because Elise had handled all the wedding preparations, Jol took responsibility for the honeymoon and planned a surprise getaway to an eco-conscious island resort area off the Australian coast. Their solar-powered accommodations provided a perfect home base for a week of snorkeling in crystal-clear waters, cooking meals together and relaxing on the beach.

THE ECO-COMFORTS OF HOME

Before or after planning your ideal organic wedding, make time to create a healthy, natural home. Choices you make when decorating, furnishing or remodeling your home can alter your health, as well as your impact on the planet. On average, we spend over half our lives inside our homes. Our overview highlights the important considerations and helps you prioritize going green in your home. From organic sheets and towels, to VOC-free paint and fair trade furnishings — you'll enjoy and benefit from eco-savvy products in your home. (See our Resources Directory for further reading <www.organicweddings.com/resources>.)

Walls, Floors, Fabrics

No matter the style or size of your home, we'll bet you have walls, floors and fabrics in it. These three basic elements can also be the source of significant chemicals and indoor air pollution. One of the major culprits here is the chemical formaldehyde, a colorless gas, which is found in many types of glue used in carpets and cabinets. Formaldehyde is also used as a finishing chemical in fabrics. Because of its prevalence in floor coverings, paints, particleboard, upholstery, window treatments and sheets, it is the most commonly found indoor toxin. To avoid breathing in formaldehyde, you can do two things: reduce the amount of the toxin you bring into your home and increase the amount of fresh air circulated within your home. On average, indoor air is at least three times more polluted than outdoor air, according to the EPA. Two additional chemicals that cause damage to health and the environment are PVC plastics and dioxin. Avoid bringing these and other air polluting toxins into your home by minimizing anything made

WOW — WHY ORGANIC WEDDINGS?

Conventionally-grown cotton is a major culprit in polluting the environment — using fully 25% of the world's insecticides and 10% of the world's pesticides, although the crop accounts for only 2-3% of the world's cultivated land. Pesticides can cause serious health problems in farm workers, and over time they actually decrease the fertility of topsoil. If those facts don't convince you, consider that the cotton crop finds its way into our food chain, in the form of cottonseed oil and high-protein cottonseed meal, which is fed to livestock and poultry. In fact, cotton fiber accounts for only 35% of a field's yield; 60% is cottonseed.

using glues and fabrics that have been heavily treated and finished. Paint is also a culprit. Conventional paints continue to "off gas" for years after being applied, so be sure to use low and no-VOC paints. Fortunately, many top paint companies are now making high-quality eco-friendly paints. (See box on page 138.)

Fun with Fabrics: A variety of fabrics are found in every room in the house. This provides a great opportunity to incorporate natural and organic fibers throughout your home: for window treatments, bedding, bath linens, table linens, upholstery, and throw rugs. There are many types of natural fibers, including green cotton, organic cotton, industrial hemp, silk, organic wool, alpaca, Tencel, linen/flax and others. Synthetic fabrics and synthetic blends should be minimized wherever possible because they are derived from petroleum. The process of extracting, refining and transporting fossil fuels has severe

Candlelight not only saves energy, it casts a beautiful glow to an evening event.

negative effects on our environment. Polyester, polar fleece and acrylic are all petroleum-based fabrics created by spinning plastic into fibers. Buying these fabrics increases the demand for oil-based products. Also, synthetics do not let your skin breathe in the same way natural fibers do. While hi-tech synthetic fibers, like Thinsulate, are useful for certain applications, the reality is that on a day-to-day basis, we can drastically minimize our use of synthetics on our bodies and in our homes. As an alternative to polar fleece, try Eco-Fleece, a fleece material created by melting down plastic bottles and re-spinning the plastic into new fleece.

Most fabric dyes can create significant environmental impacts. Avoid heavily dyed clothing, which contributes to water pollution, by choosing items in their natural colors, such as green cotton (a term for conventional cotton that has not been chemically colored, bleached or treated in the finishing process). Alpaca and color-grown cotton are two fibers that are naturally colored, avoiding the need for dyes. Color-grown cotton is cultivated in earthy shades of cream, terracotta and green. Alpacas, smaller cousins to camels and llamas, are valued for their softer-than-wool coats in over 20 shades of white, black, brown and gray. For dyed items, search for those made using low-impact or natural dyes. Choosing to buy natural fibers is excellent, but you can also be eco-savvy by getting creative with what you already have. Reuse and re-sew old fabrics and clothing into unique décor items such as pillow covers, shams, table runners, place mats, napkins, patchwork quilts and more.

EARTH FRIENDLY ALTERNATIVES: WALLS AND FLOORS

- Eco-floors: Tile made from recycled glass or natural materials such as stone, cement, sustainably grown or reclaimed/recycled woods, wool carpets, grass fiber carpets (like sisal and jute), Marmoleum (a natural linoleum), and cork. (See page 172 of the Resources Directory.)

- Eco-walls: Low or no-VOC wall paints, as well as non-vinyl wallpapers applied using non-toxic glues. Companies making low and no-VOC paints include Sherwin-Williams (HealthSpec and Harmony), Benjamin Moore (EcoSpec), AFM Safecoat, EarthTech, ICI-Glidden (Ultra Hide and Lifemaster 2000). When applying paint, reduce pollution further by using brushes and rollers instead of a sprayer, which wastes more paint.

Kitchens and Bathrooms

When creating your eco-excellent kitchens and bathrooms, including laundry areas, your choices for cabinets, counters, appliances and cleaning products are ones to consider carefully:

• Cabinets should be solid wood or pressed wheat straw board. Avoid particle-board since the glues typically contain chemicals including formaldehyde.

ORGANIC CHEF NORA POUILLON ON
A Newlywed's Kitchen

We asked **Nora Pouillon** (see page 88 for her interview) to give us her advice on setting up a newlywed's kitchen — how to choose the right items to streamline preparing those great home-cooked organic meals, while bearing budget and space in mind. Here are her suggestions:

"For cookware, you only need a few key pieces: a good frying pan, a middle-size pot to sauté vegetables or make stews, a larger pot to cook pasta or use as a steamer, and a pressure cooker. Pressure cookers are good because they protect the nutrients. They are really not hard to use. I also suggest a simple food processor or blender, and a good knife. That's all you need to get started and cook some wonderful meals together.

If you purchase or register for cookware and kitchen items, start with good ones. I use only stainless steel cookware; no aluminum or other surfaces. Stainless steel is best because it doesn't react with any foods, heats evenly and cleans easily. I avoid Teflon or anything made from petroleum. If a Teflon surface begins to break down from scratches, get rid of it — otherwise you are eating it when it mixes with your food.

The old-fashioned cast-iron frying pans are wonderful. You can use them for everything. They conduct heat evenly and whatever you scrape off the pan has iron transferred to it, which is good for you. They're reasonably priced and you have them for life. You can even buy them at flea markets very cheaply and they're already seasoned. For leftovers, buy some small stainless steel containers, not plastic bags or plastic containers. Then for cleaning up after all your great organic cooking, you only need one good all-purpose, non-toxic citrus cleaner. Just dilute it in different strengths for different purposes. It works everywhere."

- Counters should be natural materials whenever possible, such as wood, stone (marble and granite) or ceramic tile. Avoid Formica and Corian, as they are synthetic.

- Choose EnergyStar <www.energystar.gov> appliances to lower energy requirements and ensure that any appliances that use water use the minimum amount possible.

- You can easily remove many chemicals from your house (without sacrificing quality) by replacing your cleaning products with non-toxic and biodegradable formulas. Avoid chlorine and phosphates. Try Seventh Generation, Earth-friendly and Ecover products.

Reduce the energy it takes to run your home, which will save a huge amount of air pollution as well as 10-90 percent on your utility bills. Many energy-conserving measures are easy and inexpensive to take. For ideas, check out Rocky Mountain Institute <www.rmi.org> or the US Department of Energy <www.eere.energy.gov/consumer-info>. Once you've done your best to conserve energy around your home, you may be able to switch to a utility that lets you choose to buy energy generated from renewable sources. Where this option isn't available, you can still buy Tradeable Renewable Certificates from a company that is certified by Green-e <www.green-e.org>, an independent verification program. You still pay your regular utility bill, but also pay a small premium to a renewable-energy supplier that is replacing the kilowatts you draw from the national energy grid with clean energy. Non-renewable electricity sources are the number one cause of industrial air pollution.

Bedrooms and Living Rooms

Being eco-minded in places where we relax and recharge is especially important. Since almost a third of each day is spent in your bed, choosing to have a healthy bed and chemical-free bedding is important. In our living rooms, decorating with natural fabrics is key. If you must use conventional fabrics, then keep them to a minimum. Don't choose to have any additional finishing sprays and ventilate well for the first six months you own the furniture or window treatments.

Incandescent lighting is extremely inefficient, putting out more heat than light. According to *The Better World Handbook*, fluorescent lights last about ten times longer and use one-quarter the energy. You can buy compact fluorescent bulbs now that look just like incandescents, don't flicker or hum, and can be used with dimmers. They cost more up front (about $11-12) but save an average of $75 over the bulb's lifetime. If you replace 25% of the highly-used light bulbs in your home with efficient fluorescents, you could save about 50% on your lighting energy bill. (Source: CA Energy Commission.) You can even buy full-spectrum compact fluorescent bulbs, which give off a pleasing, eye-refreshing light that imitates natural sunshine.

Congratulations on making your home healthier and more eco-friendly. Remember the last step for any renovation or remodeling is the proper disposal and clean-up of any and all materials. Contact your local municipal waste department for guidelines in your area.

CLEARING THE AIR

Investing in an air filtration or purification system is a good idea. However, residential air purifiers are generally not powerful enough to remove gaseous pollutants. So, unless you live in a very polluted area, opening the windows is the best way to clear the air. While pollutants such as radon need their own special mitigation systems, exposure to air pollution generated from new wallpaper, paint, floors and fabrics is hard to filter out. Consider a HEPA vacuum to capture small particles. Use a dehumidifier to avoid problems with mold — a potentially potent indoor air problem. Mother Nature's answer to better air is green plants. NASA studies confirm that certain plants — like Boston ferns, English ivy and peace lilies — are quite effective at absorbing household toxins.

SHINING A LIGHT ON
Candles

Burning candles in your home creates soft light and a warm, cozy feel. Candles can also be used for aromatherapy, which scents the air with relaxing or invigorating aromas. However, not all candles will give you peace of mind. Most mass-market candles are made from paraffin wax, a petroleum by-product. Besides being a non-renewable resource, this type of wax can contain up to 11 documented toxins, including two carcinogens known to the EPA; benzene and toluene. Trendy gel candles are made with petroleum jelly and pose the same concerns.

The healthy alternative is to choose all-natural beeswax or soy wax candles, which are made from renewable resources. Beeswax produces far less soot than ordinary candles — up to 95% less. Also, avoid candlewicks with wire cores. If this wire is made from lead, burning the candle can be a health hazard, especially for young children. Lead-cored wicks have been banned in the US (since 1974), but may still be used in imported candles, especially from countries where health standards are less reliable. To be safe, choose candles with all natural cotton or hemp wicks.

Be choosy about scented candles, too. The fragrance oils used to scent ordinary candles contain artificial chemicals. Like perfumes (see page 39), these fragrances are not regulated and few have been rigorously tested for adverse health effects. If you're looking for candles that will give off a pleasing scent, select those made with genuine essential oils rather than chemical fragrances.

For earth- and health-friendly candles, check out:

- Way Out Wax
  <www.wayoutwax.com>
- Jenni Originals
  <www.jennioriginals.com>
- Bee Natural
  <www.beenatural.com>
- Pacifica Candles
  <www.pacificacandles.com>

GREENER MONEY

Finances and Socially Responsible Investing

Put your money where your values are — it is one of the most powerful tools an individual has to make a difference in the world. While wedding expenditures are short-term, investing with your values lets you take advantage of compounded interest over time to truly effect change in your community and the world. Just as Organic Weddings' message begins with harnessing the power of the nuptial purse to do good, so too does socially responsible investing on a much broader scale. As newlyweds who may be combining finances, this time in your life presents a valuable opportunity to re-evaluate your financial strategies together.

For our discussion on greening your finances, Organic Weddings has drawn detailed information and notable inspiration from three recognized experts in the area of Socially Responsible Investing (SRI): Hal Brill, Jack A. Brill and Cliff Feigenbaum. Their book, *Investing with Your Values* is a treasure trove for anyone interested in learning more about aligning your money with your values.

What is Socially Responsible Investing?

While most people would tell you they want to leave a cleaner, more peaceful world for their children to grow up in, the conventional wisdom of Wall Street tends to tell us to leave those values at home. Chasing profit rules the day, and financial advisors would have us confine our social and environmental concerns to the arena of charitable giving, or worse — we come to believe these concerns will cloud our otherwise sound investment judgment. This leaves many people feeling torn between making money and making a difference in the world with their investment choices. But does it have to be this way?

Socially responsible investing is an ever-expanding movement that is becoming more mainstream every day. It is a rising tide of pension fund managers, Wall Street analysts, and ordinary people at home just checking their stocks on the Web, who are all convinced that ethics and finances do mix, and do so in many profitable ways.

> " Two goals — personal consistency and advancing corporate social responsibility — work together to shape the ways in which we invest with values. But generally, it is the first goal that creates awareness of the underlying issues.
> — Amy Domini "

A Short History of Socially Responsible Investing

Various religious groups are among the first credited with socially responsible investing or values-based investing. On the basis of their beliefs, many refused to put their money into "sinful" enterprises such as casinos, liquor stores, weapons makers, or businesses that mistreated workers. Fast-forward to the tumultuous 1960s, when issues like civil rights, the environment and nuclear power filtered onto the evening news and into the consciousness of mainstream America. Especially important was the realization that these social and environmental issues were connected to economic power — and from this fertile ground the first real handful of socially-screened investments sprouted in the 1970s and 80s. The Pax World mutual fund, Dreyfus Third Century, Calvert, Working Assets, and Parnassus were trailblazers.

One of the proudest moments of the SRI movement to date was the remarkable influence wielded by investors through the 1980s against the apartheid system in South Africa. Starting in the late 1960s, students began demanding that universities stop investing in a country where white and black citizens were required to live in separate residential districts, a tactic used to repress the black majority. Through the 1970s, US cities and states began to declare they would not invest in companies tied to the South African economy. Socially responsible mutual funds screened out investments in South Africa, and in 1986 the US government officially passed sanctions against doing business with the country. Unable to withstand these economic pressures, the government of F.W. de Klerk began reforms in 1989. By 1990, Nelson Mandela walked free from prison.

Throughout the 1990s, values-based investing had gained a foothold with individuals and institutions alike. Today, old myths and concerns that ethical investing meant lower returns — have been thoroughly debunked. Every day, millions of people around the world succeed at putting their finances in step with their values.

Welcome to the Driver's Seat

In a global economy where billions of dollars fly at light-speed around the world every day, it is easy to see the financial marketplace as a mysterious and impersonal system. You might think of your investments as a tiny drop in the bucket, and become convinced that the labor practices or environmental track record of a multinational corporation are beyond reach. As we saw in 2002 with the corporate scandals from Enron to Worldcom, corporate responsibility and accountability are lacking. But take heart, because it is this very lever of corporate power that can give you, the socially responsible investor, the advantage. Shareholders, as owners of corporations, have a powerful opportunity to express their values through their financial decisions.

While a number of large corporations rival governments in terms of power and influence, there is a growing understanding of how this economic power affects the environment and the fabric of communities both at home and abroad. In our economic system, where mergers and acquisitions concentrate power into fewer and fewer corporate headquarters, all may seem lost for local communities and for commerce that protects people and the planet. However, this is exactly where Hal Brill, Jack A. Brill and Cliff Feigenbaum, the authors of *Investing with Your Values*, take their cue:

"Once people understand that corporations are making most decisions of consequence in our society, they will look for ways to have influence. A company can be influenced in several ways: by its customers, its workforce, community pressure, governmental action, or its investors. Of these, investment is the only strategy to offer Americans the right to sit at the table, to be an insider and work for change."

According to a 2001 study conducted by the Social Investment Forum, $2.3 trillion in assets are under management in the US in socially and environmentally responsible portfolios — an increase of 97 percent since the Forum's 1997 study. This means that nearly one out of every eight dollars invested in America is part of a socially conscious portfolio. This number further breaks down as follows:

• $1.5 trillion is invested using Avoidance and/or Affirmative Screening.

• $906 billion is in assets controlled by investors who play an active role in share-holder advocacy.

• $7.6 billion is dedicated to community investments.

According to Lipper, a leading provider of mutual fund information and analysis, the first nine months of 2001 saw a 94 percent drop in the dollars that investors put into all mutual funds, compared to only a 54 percent drop for socially screened funds. Between January and June 2002, the value of assets in socially responsible mutual funds *increased* by 3%, whereas the assets of US diversified funds *decreased* by 9.5%. The data also show that in June 2002, an especially tumultuous period in which the S&P 500 lost over 13 percent, socially responsible mutual funds benefited from net *inflows* of $47 million, while US diversified funds suffered from net *redemptions* of nearly $13 billion. These trends illustrate that social investors tend to see beyond short-term fluctuations and look for long-term gains in stable, growing companies, avoiding the "what did you do for me this quarter?" mentality that pervades many investors and forces companies to look for immediate sources of profits, many times at the expense of environmental or social issues.

Getting Started

Being a newlywed presents an opportune time to align personal values and beliefs with personal finances for more rewarding investments. Socially responsible investing is more accessible than you may have realized. Community banking options are available to investors starting with only $50. Even one person's money can make a difference, no matter how small. So, learn more and get involved — invest wisely for your future together and for the planet. Vote with your dollars and play a critical role influencing the direction of our society for generations to come.

To get started with socially responsible investing, consider these steps:

1. Financial Check-up: Review your current financial situation and design a financial plan that will help you achieve your goals in life. If you are in considerable debt, you should first consider how to best pay off money owed in relation to your income.

2. Values Check-in: Clarify your personal values and define how you want to relate to the social, environmental and ethical issues of our times. Determine your goals for investing with your values.

3. Investment Strategy Choices: Decide how you want to strategically evaluate companies or industries in order to achieve your values-based investment goals. You can practice Avoidance Screening, Affirmative Screening, Community Investing and Shareholder Activism (see box on page 148 for details on these strategies). You might also decide to support companies that are moving toward more sustainable practices in response to consumer pressure — Home Depot, Starbucks and Staples, for example — and then contact a company investor relations representative to let them know the reason for your investment.

4. Design your Natural Portfolio: Select specific investments that will enable you to both make money and make a difference. This is also a time to consider if employing the services of a financial professional would be advantageous, but be sure to seek recommendations from trusted sources and interview multiple candidates.

5. Change your Life: Review your spending patterns and employment situation in light of your values. Make adjustments such as reducing consumption, creating your right livelihood and supporting causes that you believe in. In *Your Money or Your Life*, authors Vicki Robin and Joe Dominguez offer a guide to taking a hard look at the trade-offs we make between earning money and enjoying our work and free time. It's a great starting point for taking stock of our habits with money.

6. Invigorate your Community: Bring values-based investing into your community through participation in initiatives that strengthen local economies.

7. Heal the Economic System: Become a player in redesigning the global economic and political system so that it better reflects humane and sustainable values.

(Adapted from "The Seven Steps of Natural Investing," Natural Investing, Inc., <www.naturalinvesting.com>.)

FOUR STRATEGIES FOR
Values-Based Investing

Avoidance Screening: Avoid investing in companies or industries that engage in businesses that you do not support. Examples could include alcohol production, environmental pollution, excessive executive pay, gambling or casino operations, genetic engineering and GMOs, global warming, nuclear power, repressive regimes, sweatshops and child labor, toxic products, tobacco production, weapons contractors and the military, workplace discrimination.

Affirmative Screening: Intentionally invest in companies or industries that engage in businesses that you support. Examples could include affordable housing, animal welfare, clean transportation, community development, education, energy conservation, environmental clean-up, green real estate, indigenous peoples' rights, job creation, natural food and healthy products, progressive workplace policies, renewable energy, recycling, tree savers/substitutes.

Community Investing: Invest your dollars with banks and other financial institutions that create opportunities for economically disadvantaged people in the US and overseas who are underserved by traditional banking systems. It can be as easy as which bank you choose for your checking account, and works to revitalize local communities.

Shareholder Activism: Directly influence companies' corporate policies by advocating for businesses to consider the "triple bottom line" — people, planet and profits: making profits while being a steward of environmental and social responsibility.

(Adapted from Brill, Brill and Feigenbaum's "Natural Investing Wheel.")

EATING FOR HEALTH AND HAPPINESS

Sitting down to eat together is a simple pleasure to be savored. Whether you're around your own kitchen table or dining out, there are plenty of opportunities to make choices in favor of more sustainable eating habits. If you're planning on starting a family, you may be especially interested in the health benefits of eating organic, whole foods. Educate yourself about where your food comes from. A major part of natural living is what we eat, but you may be surprised at what you learn about the environment and economics on the path from farm to table.

What's In: Eating Seasonally and Locally

It's only natural to feel drawn to eat what's in season. It's often what looks freshest in the grocery store or it's what we crave depending on the weather: a hearty stew on a cold winter night or cool, refreshing fruits and vegetables in the summer. Research confirms that eating seasonally is a healthy idea. From a nutrient standpoint, it's all downhill from the time produce is picked out of the field, so better to fill your basket with what's fresh than eat out-of-season items that have been sitting in storage.

Eating with the seasons also makes sense for the environment. Whatever is locally abundant did not have to travel for miles in a refrigerated truck or be flown in from even more distant places. Fresh mangoes in the dead of winter may not come cheap, but even that price does not include the costs to the environment of burning fossil fuels to ship that produce far from where it was picked. According to Cynthia Barstow's book, *The Eco-Foods Guide*, an authoritative guide to healthy eating, only 10% of the total fossil fuels used in agriculture are spent producing the food. The other 90% goes to shipping, packaging, and marketing. While the seasons for different produce will vary depending on your local growing season, see Alice Waters' Chez Panisse Calendar of Seasonal Eating on page 159.

Your Next Trip Down the Aisle

Your typical mega-supermarket aims to please. A strawberry can be had in the dead of winter, or maybe you'll get your hands on a watermelon imported from a country where they're having summer. Shopping with a mind to both your own health and the environment's may seem to make the choices even harder. So, we'll arm you with some guidelines to remember as you prowl the aisles in search of balance and buying habits that your checkbook can handle. Step one in this journey is to become an avid label reader. The power of voting with your dollars depends on having enough information to make an informed choice.

Choose Organic (and Biodynamic): This means food grown or raised without the use of synthetic pesticides or fertilizers, antibiotics, or sewage sludge (often used as fertilizer); not irradiated, and free from genetic engineering. Products labeled "organic" must meet or exceed the standards passed by the USDA in October 2002. Organic farmers rotate crops to outwit pests, plant cover crops to keep down weeds, or enrich the soil with compost instead of applying fertilizers. Besides keeping chemicals and toxic residues out of your food, organics keep these things out of our soil and water. Ultimately, organic is about farming in a way that protects the health of a whole ecosystem — including the soil, insects and wildlife, and the people who tend and harvest the field.

Biodynamic is organic and then some. The biodynamic growing approach regards the earth as a vital, nourishing organism, and takes care to restore and renew the soil by planting and harvesting during specific calendar cycles.

Be Good to Bugs: If organic isn't available, or is beyond your budget at times, consider purchasing items from transitional farms or farms using the Integrated Pest Management (IPM) approach. Whereas a conventional farm often sprays for insects or disease on a pre-arranged schedule, whether the crops need it or not, IPM farms will check the fields first and adjust their strategies appropriately. Food grown on these farms is not certified as organic, but is more natural since farmers make a real effort to reduce the chemicals applied to food crops. For example, rather than spraying for cer-

WOW — WHY ORGANIC WEDDINGS?

Besides getting out of our SUVs, the non-partisan Union of Concerned Scientists has concluded that eating less meat is an important action Americans can take to help the environment. Meat production causes more environmental harm than any other food production. It's been estimated that growing a pound of wheat requires 60 pounds of water, while producing a pound of beef takes 2,500-6,000 pounds of water. It also takes at least 5 pounds of grain fed to cattle to produce one pound of beef. That's why 70% of the grain and soybeans we grow in this country is fed to animals, rather than being consumed directly — despite persistent worldwide problems with hunger and malnutrition and claims that genetically-engineered crops are the only answer to the world's food "shortage." Eating lower on the food chain more regularly is also better, because growing evidence shows environmental chemicals also accumulate in the fatty tissues of animals and fish.

tain pests, they might release ladybugs onto a field and let nature do its thing. A "transitional" farm is one making the switch to organic but which has yet to be certified, proving that its soil is free of certain toxic residues and pesticides.

Avoid Additives and Antibiotics: From sugar and salt to preservatives and colorings, you could fill a dictionary with the often-unpronounceable additives found in food on supermarket shelves. Some (saccharin, monosodium glutamate or MSG) have been known to cause cancer in laboratory tests. Find out the relative risks of 73 common food additives from the Center for Science in the Public Interest at <www.cspinet.org>.

A related concern is the hormones and antibiotics that are commonly given to farm animals, which show up in both dairy products and meat. A growth hormone called rBGH or BST is often used to boost milk production, and pasteurization does not eliminate it. This is especially troublesome in kids, whose natural hormone-led development could be affected. Likewise, factory-farm animals are kept pumped full of antibiotics to prevent outbreaks of disease. Under healthy conditions, antibiotics should be given to animals as a last resort. So look for labels saying your dairy and meat products are free from antibiotics and rBGH/BST.

Avoid Genetically Modified Organisms (GMOs): This means the genetic building-blocks of the product you're eating have been manipulated in a lab to create supposedly beneficial properties such as resistance to disease — but at unknown risk of creating allergens and potentially creating "superweeds" and "superpests." What many consumers don't realize is that they've already signed up to participate in this grand experiment, since the US government refuses to require safety testing or labeling for genetically-modified foods. Consumer backlash against GMOs in other countries has been fierce, especially in Europe. In the US, however, the Organic Consumers Association asserts that 60-75 percent of non-

If you're new to reading labels, don't worry about trying to sort it all out at once. Two great websites to help you navigate through the maze are <www.eco-label.org> and <www.responsibleshopper.org>, which will tell you what you need to know when you see tiny print.

Eco-Foods Guide's Top Ten Considerations when Shopping

1. Where is it from? (Local, regional, another country?)

2. How was it grown? (Organic, IPM, biodynamic, shade-grown?)

3. Was it grown by a big agribusiness or small family farm?

4. Is it in season?

5. Could I buy this closer to the farmer? (Farmers' markets, farmstands, CSA?)

6. Does it contain GMOs?

7. Were antibiotics or growth hormones used? (Factory raised or free-range?)

8. Is it fairly traded and/or sustainably sourced?

9. How was it processed or preserved?

10. Is it consistent with my personal values?

Reprinted with permission from *The Eco-Foods Guide*, by Cynthia Barstow.

organic supermarket foods now contain some genetically-modified ingredients. The only way to be sure you're not bringing home these altered foods is to buy organic, which prohibits genetic modification.

Find Fair Trade and Free Range: You'll most likely see the term "Fair Trade" associated with coffee, tea or cocoa. It means that farmers have received a reasonable price for their crop, enabling them to stay out of debt and poverty (see page 82 for more information). When it comes to animals raised for food, fair and humane treatment is still a major problem. Look for free range poultry and meat, and consider everything from fishing practices that needlessly entrap other species to whether farm raised meat — hogs, chicken, cattle, fish and more — are living cruelty-free lives before making their way to your plate.

Back to the Farm

Finding food closer to the field is getting easier. Around the country, farmer's markets, community supported agriculture (CSAs), urban gardens and the like are keeping our tables brimming with the freshest, most in-season produce available — eliminating the middlemen and reducing transportation impact between you and the farm. Some farmers' markets stick to fresh produce, while others have local meats, cheeses, bread, preserves and plants. Farmers' markets operate in most cities and many suburbs. CSAs allow families or individuals to buy shares, which entitle them to a weekly box of peak season farm-fresh goodies. By paying your share up front, farmers are guaranteed an income, are spared the ups and downs of produce prices, can make long-term investments in ecological practices, and escape the rat race of industrial agribusiness. However, it won't take long before the eco-conscious shopper faces a tough choice: what if local isn't organic? Although we can't make the decision for you, base your choice on what's most important to you. Maybe you live in a rural area, and see farmland being rapidly snapped up by developers — supporting local farms might be your preference. On the other hand, if taking a stand against pesticides is on the top of your list, you may choose to always buy organic no matter what the transportation costs to get it to you.

GOOD BREEDING

Kelmscott Rare Breeds Foundation <www.kelmscott.org> in Lincolnville, Maine, is an educational farm that raises over 150 animals from 20 breeds of rare and endangered livestock. Some would call it a Noah's Ark of farm animals, preserving species that will be lost to the earth forever if not conserved. Before the rise of modern industrial agriculture, farm animals came from a wide gene pool and this biodiversity protected the stocks from large-scale genetic catastrophe. Now, however, many rare farm breeds are in danger of extinction due to the selective breeding practices of factory farms. Letting centuries of natural biodiversity and careful breeding become channeled into a few selected breeds is dangerous, as genetically-similar populations are more prone to outbreaks of disease. Additionally, Kelmscott's care and concern for these unique and valuable animals ensures that important knowledge won't be lost to future generations.

The bride is wearing
a sqaure neck
hemp/silk ball gown
with a silk shawl.

EATING OUT

Sure, you can control your cupboards, but how about when you leave the nest? Fear not, because organic and seasonal eating doesn't have to end at your doorstep. The options for healthy eating outside of your home are expanding...

Chefs Collaborative: A growing network of chefs and restaurateurs is committed to creating delicious meals from local, seasonal ingredients. They publish a handy wallet-sized *Guide to Good Eating,* a nationwide restaurant locator of network members. Chefs Collaborative <www.chefscollaborative.org> members promote sustainable cuisine by designing menus that highlight pure foods, and by supporting local organic farms and ranches with their business.

Slow Food: From Italy, where a love affair with food is well established, comes the Slow Food <www.slowfood.com> movement, an emerging international culture that encourages the savoring and celebration of good food, regional cuisines and the warmth of spirited company around the table. In reaction to the hectic pace of modern eating habits, epitomized in the book *Fast Food Nation,* by Eric Schlosser, Slow Food invites us to enjoy the everyday pleasures of food. You can join a local chapter, meet like minded foodies and attend fun events like gourmet dinners and farm tours.

O'Naturals: A pioneering alternative to standard fast food is emerging in the Northeast. The idea is that as much as we'd like to slow down and celebrate every meal, many regularly rely on the convenience of fast(er) food. O'Naturals, <www.onaturals.com> currently in Maine and Massachusetts, is unapologetically fast, but serves up healthy, organic and locally-grown items on its menu, like hormone-free chicken nuggets, sandwiches and more.

The Green Restaurant Association: An Internet eco-eating destination for those in southern California is Dine Green <www.dinegreen.com>, run by the Green Restaurant Association. The restaurants, cafes and other members in this directory have pledged not to use Styrofoam containers and to work towards 11 other principles of membership, such as recycling, waste reduction, use of organics and energy efficiency. Right now it's a budding local effort, but look for new members being added nationwide.

Words of Wisdom

Stonyfield Farm's story is inspiring – from humble beginnings as an organic farm school project with a great yogurt recipe to the number three yogurt brand in the US with nearly $100 million in annual sales. At the heart and soul of that journey sits Gary Hirshberg, whose strong belief that all companies can be environmental and social stewards keeps him at the forefront of values-based business models and socially responsible investing. His mantra, "business is the most powerful force on the planet" is integral to his strategies for Stonyfield and O'Naturals, a new natural fast foods restaurant of which he is a co-founder and Chairman. Gary was also co-Chair from 1993-97 of the Social Venture Network and is the founder of the Social Venture Institute.

Organic Weddings: Who or what shaped your life with respect to the values we see in your company and career?

Gary Hirshberg: My mother was a big influence. As a single mom with five kids who ran her own business, she said we needed to be dedicated to some type of service because there were always people in greater need than us. My father, an entrepreneur, ran a shoe company, but also was unconsciously part of a legacy of pollution. Through him, I came to see business as the source of all pollution, but I also saw that business had the power to do good. My father's factory was the central employer for the small town it was in. When they had to move manufacturing offshore, I watched an entire community go through a tragic and dramatic change. I realized that most of what goes on in the environment is a result of us being unconscientious, but that it is easy to integrate a commitment to the environment into what we do. Growing up in New Hampshire also influenced me. You could stand on top of Mt. Washington and watch the air quality change almost annually. When I was a kid, you could often see the ocean from the top. No one has seen the ocean from up there in years.

OW: Two significant changes in the world of organics are often debated: the USDA regulations and the trend of corporate investment in smaller, organic brands. ☞

Words of Wisdom (contd.)

☞ **How has your experience colored your thoughts on these issues?**

GH: To me the investment by large companies into small entities, or Heinz launching organic ketchup, are positive events. Cynics will say, "Oh, it's terrible that big business is getting in." But we aren't going to change the world if we don't change these companies. Their influence on millions, if not billions of people is undeniable. People who buy organic products have stopped the pollution of tens of thousands of acres; thousands of farm workers and their families are no longer being exposed to poisonous pesticides. Food is healthier. Wildlife species are returning. Topsoil is improving. We don't have the time to sit around, because even if we stopped all carbon emissions today it would still be 30 years before we'd see a reversal of global warming. If we stopped using all pesticides today, it would still be 30 or 40 years before all the toxins would degrade. We can't be too proud or too exclusive. Ultimately the day that organic goods are on every supermarket shelf and in Sears is the day that I'll know we have succeeded.

OW: What is something you do in your own home to reduce your ecological footprint?

GH: The thing I'm proudest about is how we constructed our super-insulated home. This house is about twice the size of our old house, but we cut our energy requirements (and our heating bill) by half. What we did may be more effective in new construction, but retrofitting through attention to windows, walls and doorways saves an amazing amount of energy. I used to build windmills, so I believe in alternative energies, but today, the quickest payback is conservation and plugging the leaks.

OW: Why organic weddings?

GH: Taking care of the planet is just a state of mind. Most environmental problems exist because people haven't thought the solutions are a priority. What it takes is having a hopeful attitude that we can do something. And, what is a more hopeful act than a wedding? Getting married is about saying there is a future — we want to have it and we want to enjoy it together. Margaret Mead said, "Never doubt that a small group of thoughtful, committed citizens can change the world." This is the time to shine a bright light on a beautiful opportunity to have an entirely different kind of planet. 🐝

Chez Panisse

⪻ SEASONAL FOODS CALENDAR ⪼

ALICE WATERS' DEDICATION TO MENU PLANNING with seasonal ingredients is legendary. Here, she outlines a wide range of ingredients found — at certain times of the year — in Chez Panisse's extraordinary menus. This list is based on availability in Northern California; however, Alice believes that with persistence it is possible to find fresh and interesting ingredients wherever you may be.

   Bon Appetit!

January

Winter lettuces (romaine, watercress, lamb's lettuce), cabbage, leeks, turnips and turnip greens, green garlic, winter squash, cardoons, artichokes, cauliflower, broccoli, rapini, celery root, parsnips, fennel, kale, *cavolo nero,* nettles, beets and beet greens, spinach, avocados, chard, chicories (escarole, Belgian endive, curly endive, radicchio, *pane di zucchero*), sweet potatoes, kohlrabi, rocket, chestnuts … winter savory, marjoram, oregano, chervil … blood oranges, kumquats, grapefruits, tangerines, pummelos, kiwifruit, lemons, loquats, mandarins, oranges, Meyer lemons, pears, apples … black truffles, chanterelles, black trumpets … crab, oysters, clams, Atlantic cod, Petrale sole, steelhead trout, Hawaiian tuna … winter pork.

February

Winter lettuces (romaine, watercress, lamb's lettuce), cabbage, leeks, turnips and turnip greens, green garlic, cardoons, artichokes, cauliflower, broccoli, rapini, celery root, parsnips, fennel, kale, *cavolo nero,* nettles, beets and beet greens, rocket, sorrel, early fava beans, spinach, curly (pepper) cress, avocados, chard, chicories (escarole, Belgian endive, curly endive, radicchio, *pane di zucchero*) … sage, marjoram, oregano, winter savory, chervil … Meyer lemons, oranges, pineapples, grapefruits, pummelos, kiwifruit, kumquats, lemons, loquats, mandarins, tangerines, oranges, pears, apples … last of the black truffles, chanterelles, black trumpets … crab, oysters, clams, Hawaiian tuna, steelhead trout, Atlantic cod … winter pork.

March

Asparagus, Belgian endive, sorrel, artichokes, fennel, cauliflower, fava beans, pea shoots, peas, snap peas, green garlic, nettles, watercress, curly cress, rocket, avocados, broccoli, rapini, cardoons, chicories (escarole, Belgian endive, curly endive, radicchio, *pane di zucchero*), leeks, mesclun lettuces, radishes, turnips and turnip greens, watercress, borage, dandelion greens … sage, cilantro, chervil … dates, grapefruit, pummelos, kiwifruit, lemons, loquats, mandarins, tangerines, oranges, pineapples, strawberries, Meyer lemons … bay scallops, crab, halibut, sand dabs, Hawaiian tuna, lobster … spring lamb, winter pork.

April

Dandelion greens, snow peas, peas, new potatoes, rocket, spring onions, amaranth greens, artichokes, asparagus, avocados, chicories (escarole, Belgian endive, curly endive), fava beans, fennel, garlic, leeks, mesclun lettuces, radishes, sorrel, turnips and turnips greens, watercress, nettles … sage, cilantro, chervil, marjoram, oregano … rhubarb, grapefruits, lemons, loquats, mandarins, tangerines, mangos, oranges, pineapple, strawberries, Meyer lemons …

morels, chanterelles ... crab, halibut, sand dabs, Hawaiian tuna, lobster ... spring lamb, winter pork.

May

Borage flowers, sugarsnap peas, baby leeks, sweet basil, spring onions, green beans, new potatoes, amaranth greens, avocados, chard, fava beans, fennel, garlic, leeks, watercress, sorrel, radishes, spinach, mesclun, rocket, dandelion greens, nettles ... sage, cilantro, basil, chervil, lavender, marjoram, oregano, dill, tarragon ... mangos, apricots, cherries, grapefruit, lemons, mandarins, tangerines, oranges, pineapples, raspberries, rhubarb, strawberries ... chanterelles, morels ... salmon, crab, lobster, halibut, sand dabs, Georgia shrimp, Hawaiian tuna ... spring lamb.

June

Green beans, summer squash and squash blossoms, corn, new garlic, amaranth greens, avocados, shell beans, beets and beet greens, chard, new chickpeas, cucumbers, fava beans, fennel, leeks, small leeks, mesclun, rocket, spinach, new onions, new potatoes, shallots, sorrel, borage ... wild fennel, summer savory, sage, cilantro, basil, chervil, lavender, marjoram, oregano, dill, tarragon ... cherries, boysenberries, olallieberries, nectarines, strawberries, peaches, apricots, blueberries, loganberries, dates, new figs, grapefruits, limes, mangos, melons, peaches, pineapples, plums, raspberries, rhubarb, strawberries ... chanterelles, morels ... salmon, crab, halibut, sand dabs, California white sea bass, Georgia shrimp, Hawaiian tuna, lobster ... grass-fed beef.

July

Cucumbers, corn, gypsy peppers, avocados, tomatoes, peas, summer squash and squash blossoms, grape leaves, Japanese eggplant, shell beans, romano beans, green beans, beets and beet greens, chard, new chickpeas, garlic, leeks, small leeks, mesclun, rocket, spinach, new onions, bell peppers, potatoes, shallots, sorrel, amaranth greens ... lavender, dill, tarragon, wild fennel, summer savory, sage, basil, chervil, cilantro ... peaches, blackberries, blueberries, apricots, boysenberries, loganberries, olallieberries, cherries, red, white and black currants, limes, mangos, melons, mulberries, nectarines, oranges, pineapples, plums, pluots, raspberries, strawberries … chanterelles … halibut, salmon, sand dabs, crab, Georgia shrimp, California white sea bass, California albacore, California swordfish, lobster … grass-fed beef.

August

Tomatoes, corn, cucumbers, sweet onions, new potatoes, shell beans, romano beans, avocados, green beans, beets and beet greens, chard, new chickpeas, eggplant, garlic, leeks, small leeks, mesclun, spinach, new onions, bell peppers and gypsy peppers, potatoes, shallots, sorrel, watercress, summer squash and squash blossoms … wild fennel, summer savory, parsley, rosemary, thyme, sage, cilantro, basil, chervil, mint, dill, tarragon, lavender, marjoram, oregano … peaches, plums, figs, grapes, sour grapes, apples, blackberries, blueberries, red, white and black currants, new dates, figs, grapefruits, huckleberries, limes, mangos, melons, mulberries, nectarines, oranges, papayas, passion fruit, pears, pineapples, pluots, raspberries, strawberries… chanterelles … salmon, halibut, Georgia shrimp, sand dabs, California white sea bass, California swordfish, California albacore, lobster … grass-fed beef.

September

Eggplant, bell peppers, tomatoes, spinach, green beans, shell beans, artichokes, avocados, beets and beet greens, chard, fennel, garlic, leeks, small leeks, mesclun, lettuce, spinach, new onions, gypsy peppers, potatoes, radishes, sorrel, watercress, summer squash and squash blossoms, nettles… wild fennel, sage, basil, chervil … grapes, figs, new walnuts, new apples, red, white and black currants, new dates, new figs, grapefruits, huckleberries, mulberries, oranges, papayas, passion fruit, peaches, pears, persimmons, plums, pluots, pomegranates, quinces, raspberries … porcini … salmon, halibut, sand dabs, Georgia shrimp, California white sea bass, California albacore, California swordfish, lobster … grass-fed beef.

October

Spinach, tomatoes, cabbage, green beans, artichokes, avocados, shell beans, beets and beet greens, broccoli, rapini, chard, chicories (escarole, Belgian endive, curly endive, radicchio, *pane di zucchero*), fennel, garlic, leeks, small leeks, mesclun,

rocket, new onions, bell peppers, potatoes, radishes, sorrel, watercress, nettles …
sage, marjoram, oregano … grapes, pears, persimmons, new apples, cranberries,
new dates, new figs, grapes, grapefruit, huckleberries, lemons, limes, oranges,
papayas, passion fruit, pomegranates, quinces, raspberries, Meyer lemons …
porcini, white truffles … Albacore tuna, Dungeness crab season begins, Georgia
shrimp, halibut, sand dabs, California white sea bass, California Albacore,
California swordfish, lobster … fall pork.

November

Winter squash, pumpkins, turnips and turnip greens, black radishes, fennel,
Belgian endive, sorrel leaves, horseradish, artichokes, avocados, beets and beet
greens, broccoli, rapini, Brussels sprouts, cabbage, cardoons, celery root, chard,
chicories (escarole, Belgian endive, curly endive, radicchio, *pane di zucchero*),
garlic, kale, leeks, small leeks, spinach, parsnips, potatoes, radishes, sorrel, sweet
potatoes, cavolo nero, nettles … sage, marjoram, oregano … winter melons,
chestnuts, persimmons, new apples, cranberries, new dates, grapefruits,
kiwifruit, oranges, passion fruit, pears, pomegranates, quinces, Meyer lemons …
white truffles, porcini, chanterelles … crab, sand dabs, California albacore, steelhead trout, Petrale sole, clams … goose, fall pork.

December

Fennel, cabbage, winter lettuces (lamb's lettuce, romaine lettuce), celery root,
kohlrabi, avocados, beets and beet greens, broccoli, rapini, Brussels sprouts, cardoons, chard, chicories (escarole, Belgian endive, curly endive, radicchio, *pane di
zucchero*), kale, leeks, spinach, parsnips, winter squash, sweet potatoes, turnips
and turnip greens, nettles, green garlic …winter savory, sage, marjoram, oregano
… tangerines, persimmons, pears, apples, cranberries, new dates, grapefruits,
pummelos, kiwifruit, kumquats, lemons, loquats, mandarins, tangerines,
oranges, pomegranates, quinces, Meyer lemons, chestnuts … black truffles, end
of white truffles, porcini, chanterelles, black trumpets …oysters, steelhead trout,
crab, cod, Petrale sole, clams, California albacore … fall pork.

(Used with permission from Chez Panisse.)

Resources Directory

In planning your wedding and beyond, explore these resources to learn more about the wide variety of good work being done to advance environmental and social issues and how your support makes a difference.

Please note that the information, goods and services offered by these organizations are suggestions only. Organic Weddings does not guarantee accuracy or quality in any way.

Recommended Reading

Periodicals:

E–The Environmental Magazine, <www.emagazine.com>

Mother Jones magazine, <www.motherjones.com>

Natural Home magazine, <www.naturalhomemagazine.com>

Organic Gardening magazine, <www.organicgardening.com>

Organic Style Magazine, <www.organicstyle.com>

Utne, <www.utne.com>

Vegetarian Times magazine, <www.vegetariantimes.com>

VegNews monthly newsletter, <www.vegnews.com>

Books:

Cynthia Barstow, *The Eco-Foods Guide*, New Society Publishers, 2002.

Hal Brill, Jack A. Brill and Cliff Feigenbaum, *Investing With Your Values*, New Society Publishers, 2000.

Michael Brower and Warren Leon, *The Consumer's Guide to Effective Environmental Choices: Practical Advice from the Union of Concerned Scientists*, Three Rivers Press, 1999.

Joe Dominguez and Vicki Robin, *Your Money or Your Life*, Penguin, 1999.

Amy Domini, *Socially Responsible Investing: Making a Difference and Making Money*, Dearborn Trade, 2001.

Ann Keeler Evans, *Promises to Keep: Crafting Your Wedding Ceremony*, Emerald Earth Publishing, 2001.

Mindy Green, *Natural Perfumes: Simple Aromatherapy Recipes,* Interweave Press, 1999.

Julia Butterfly Hill, *One Makes the Difference,* Harper Colliins, 2002.

Kat James, *The Truth About Beauty: Unlocking the Secrets of Profound Radiance*, Beyond Words, 2003.

Ellis Jones, Ross Haenfler and Brett Johnson, *The Better World Handbook*, New Society Publishers, 2001.

Kathy Keville and Mindy Green, *Aromatherapy: A Complete Guide to the Healing Art,* Ten Speed Press, 1995.

Ross A. Klein, *Cruise Ship Blues*, New Society Publishers, 2002.

Elaine Marie Lipson, *The Organic Foods Sourcebook*, McGraw Hill, 2001.

Janet Marinelli and Paul Bierman-Lytle, *Your Natural Home*, Little, Brown and Company, 1995.

Julie Forest Middleton, ed. *Songs for Earthlings — A Green Spirituality Songbook*, Emerald Earth Publishing, 1998.

Nell Newman, *The Newman's Own Organics Guide to a Good Life,* Random House, 2003.

Sheryl Nissinen, *The Conscious Bride*, New Harbinger Publications, 2000.

David Pearson, *The New Natural House Book*, Simon & Schuster, 1998.

John C. Ryan and Alan Thein Durning, *Stuff: the Secret Lives of Everyday Things*, Northwest Environment Watch, 1997.

Danny Seo, *Conscious Style Home*, St. Martin's, 2001.

Mathis Wackernagel and William Rees, *Our Ecological Footprint: Reducing Human Impact on the Earth*, New Society Publishers, 1996.

Alice Waters, *Chez Panisse Menu Cookbook*, Random House, 1982.

Katherine Whiteside, *Forcing, Etc.: The Indoor Gardener's Guide to Bringing Bulbs, Branches and Houseplants into Bloom*, Workman Publishing, 1999.

Elizabeth Zipern and Dar Williams, *The Tofu Tollbooth: A Guide to Natural Food Stores & Eating Spots*, Ceres Press, 1998.

News and Information

Capitol Reports Environmental News Link, <www.caprep.com>

Care2 Environmental Network, <www.care2.com>

Earth Day Network, <www.earthday.org>

Earth Day Resources, <www.earthdayresources.org>, 877-EARTH-46

Earth Vision, <www.earthvision.net>

Envirolink, <www.envirolink.org>

Environmental News Network, <www.enn.com>

Environment News Service, <www.ens-news.com>

GreenBiz, <www.greenbiz.com>

Planet Ark, <www.planetark.org>

Sustainable Business, <www.sustainablebusiness.com>

Awareness and Advocacy

Amnesty International <www.amnestyusa.org>

Act Green, <www.actgreen.com>

Earth Island Institute, <www.earthisland.org>

EcoPledge Campaign, <www.ecopledge.com>

EnviroHealthAction, <www.envirohealthaction.org>

Environmental Defense, <www.environmentaldefense.org>

Environmental Media Association, <www.ema-online.org>

Environmental Working Group, <www.ewg.org>

Friends of the Earth, <www.foe.org>

Greenpeace, <www.greenpeace.org>

National Council on Science and the Environment, <www.ncseonline.org>

National Resources Defense Council, <www.nrdc.org>

Physicians for Social Responsibility, <www.psr.org>

Public Citizen, <www.citizen.org>

Rocky Mountain Institute, <www.rmi.org>

The Breast Cancer Fund, <www.breastcancerfund.org>

The Union of Concerned Scientists, <www.ucsusa.org>

True Majority, <www.truemajority.org>

Working for Change, <www.giveforchange.org>

Worldwatch Institute, <www.worldwatch.org>

World Wildlife Fund, <www.worldwildlife.org>

People and Planet Friendly (Sustainable) Living

Center for a New American Dream, <www.newdream.org>

Eco Living Center, <www.ecolivingcenter.com>

Green Guide, <www.thegreenguide.com>

Green Matters, <www.greenmatters.com>

Green Sense, <www.greensense.com>

Redjellyfish, <www.redjellyfish.com>

Responsible Shopper, <www.responsibleshopper.org>

Simple Living Links, <www.onlineorganizing.com/Simple_Living_Links.htm>

Simple Living Network, <www.simpleliving.net>

Eco-Beauty and Fashion

Aveda, <www.aveda.com>

BeesWork, <www.beeswork.com>, 415-883-5660

Benedetta, <www.benedetta.com>, 888-868-8331

Brides Against Breast Cancer, <www.makingmemories.org>

Chestnut and Bay, <www.chestnutandbay.com>, 877-962-4923

coolnotcruel, <www.coolnotcruel.com>

Co-op America's Guide to Ending Sweatshops, <www.sweatshops.org>

Dr. Hauschka, <www.drhauschka.com>, 800-247-9907

Fair Trade Federation, <www.fairtradefederation.org>, 202-872-5329

Fresh Unlimited, <www.freshunlimited.com>, 866-326-2111

Indigenous Designs, <www.indigenousdesigns.com>, 707-571-7811

Jane Iredale Mineral Cosmetics, <wwwjaneiredale.com>, 800-817-5665

John Masters Organics, <www.johnmasters.com>, 212-343-9590

Lavera, <www.lavera-usa.com>, 877-528-3727

Mandy Aftel/Aftelier, <www.aftelier.com>, 510-841-2111

Mega Food Vitamins, <www.megafood.com>, 800-848-2542

Moo Shoes, <www.mooshoes.com>, 212-481-5792

National Labor Committee for Worker and Human Rights, <www.nlcnet.org>,
   212-242-3002

Patagonia, <www.patagonia.com>, 800-638-6464

Rawganique (for Ecolution), <www.rawganique.com>,
   866-RAW HEMP (729-4367)

Sweat X, <www.sweatx.net>

Terressentials, <www.terressentials.com>, 301-371-7333

The Bridal Garden, <www.bridalgarden.org>

The Coalition for Consumer Information on Cosmetics, <www.leapingbunny.org>

The Glass Slipper Project, <www.glassslipperproject.org>

Under the Canopy, <www.underthecanopy.com>, 888-CANOPY-9

Wildlife Works,<www.wildlife-works.com>, 415-332-8081

Jewelry

"Diamonds, the Real Story," *National Geographic*, March 2002

Amnesty International Clean Diamonds <www.amnestyusa.org/diamonds>

Apollo Diamond, <www.apollodiamond.com>

Canadia Diamonds, <www.canadia.com>

Gemesis Cultured Diamonds, <www.gemesis.com>

Green Karat, <www.greenkarat.com>

Global Witness, <www.globalwitness.org/campaigns/diamonds>

Sirius Diamonds, <www.siriusdiamonds.com>

"The New Diamond Age," *Wired,* September 2003

Trees and Tree-Free

Carbon Neutral Network, <www.carbonneutral.com>

Conservatree, <www.conservatree.com>, 415-721-4230

Forest Stewardship Council, <www.fscus.org>, 877-372-5646

Global ReLeaf, <www.americanforests.org>/planttrees>

Heifer Project International, <www.heifer.org>, 800-422-0474

Living Tree Paper Company, <www.livingtreepaper.com>, 800-309-3974

MarryMe Woods at Future Forests, <www.futureforests.com>

ReThink Paper, <www.rethinkpaper.com>

The Markets Initiative, <www.oldgrowthfree.com>/industry_leaders.html>

Trees for the Future, <www.treesftf.org>, 800-643-0001

Twisted Limb Paperworks, <www.twistedlimbpaper.com>

Ceremony and Traditions

Heart Scroll, <www.heartscroll.com>

Local Harvest, <www.localharvest.com>

MUSE, <www.musemusic.org>

Occasional Words, <www.occasionalwords.com>

Rite to Remember, <www.aritetoremember.com>

River Prayers, <www.riverprayers.org>

Songs from You to Yours, <www.songsfromyoutoyours.com>, 877-999-SONG

Universal Life Church, <www.ulc.org>

Verse It, <www.verseit.com>

Renewable/Green Energy

3 Phases Energy, <www.3phases.com>, 415-346-7662

American Council for an Energy Efficient Economy, <www.aceee.org>

Energy Star,<www.energystar.gov>, 888-STAR-YES

Full Spectrum Solutions, <www.fullspectrumsolutions.com>, 888-574-7014

Green Mountain Energy, <www.greenmountain.com>, 800-286-5856

Green-e, <www.green-e.org>, 888-63-GREEN

Native Energy's Windbuilder Program, <www.nativeenergy.com>, 800-924-6826

Renewable Choice Energy, <www.renewablechoice.com>, 303-652-0770

Flowers

Diamond Organics, <www.diamondorganics.com>, 888-674-2642

Keuka Flower Farm, <www.driedflowersdirect.com>

Organic Bouquet, <www.organicbouquet.com>

Purple Pastures Lavender Farm, <www.purplepastures.com/Weddings.cfm>

TulipWorld, <www.tulipworld.com>

Victorian Bride, <www.victorianbride.com>, 800-706-4050

Wedding Herbs, <www.weddingherbs.com>

Wedding Petals, <www.weddingpetals.com>

Women's Organic Flower Enterprise, <www.homelessgardenproject.org/wofc.html>

Favors

Chocolate Necessities, <www.chocolatenecessities.com>, 800-804-0589

Dagoba Organic Chocolate, <www.dagobachocolate.com>, 541-664-9030

Direct Access International, <www.directaccessintl.com>, 800-811-7383

Ecoparti, <www.ecoparti.com>

Evergreen Memories, <www.evergreenmemories.ca>

Favor Boutique, <www.favorboutique.com/earthfriendly.html>, 866-929-4184

Favors by Serendipity, <www.favorsbyserendipity.com>, 800-320-2664

GreenWorld Project, <www.greenworldproject.net>

Jubilee Chocolates, <www.jubileechocolates.com>, 800-747-4808

Lavender Green, <www.lavendergreen.com>, 703-684-4433

North American Butterfly Association, <www.naba.org>

Plant A Memory, <www.plantamemory.com>, 888-315-7333

Seeds of Change, <www.seedsofchange.com>, 888-762-7333

The National Arbor Day Foundation, <www.arborday.org/gifttrees>

Gifts and Registries

"Tied to a Cause" from Vineyard Vines, <www.vineyardvines.com>, 800-892-4982

Aid to Artisans, <www.aidtoartisans.org>, 860-947-3344

American Institute of Philanthropy, <www.charitywatch.org>

Better Business Bureau Wise Giving Alliance, <www.give.org>

Childsake, <www.childsake.com>, 360-752-1211

Co-op America's National Green Pages, <www.greenpages.org>

Eco Express, <www.ecoexpress.com>, 800-733-3495

Eco Golf, <www.ecogolf.com>, 888-326-3003

Eco-artware.com, <www.eco-artware.com>, 877-326-2781

Eziba, <www.eziba.com>, 888-404-5108

Fair Trade Federation, <www.fairtradefederation.com>

Fresh Air Fund, <www.freshair.org>, 800-367-0003

I Do Foundation, <www.idofoundation.org>

iGive.com, <www.igive.com>

Kelmscott Rare Breeds Foundation, Adopt an Animal, <www.kelmscott.org>, 207-763-4088

Married for Good, <www.marriedforgood.com>

Nova Natural Toys and Crafts, <www.novanatural.com>

Novica—Global Artisans, <www.novica.com>

Organic Weddings, <www.organicweddings.com>

Rent Mother Nature, <www.rentmothernature.com>, 800-232-4048

Shop for Change, <www.workingforchange.com/shop/>

Sunrise Pashmina, <www.sunrise-pashmina.com>, FAX only 708-575-6620

Ten Thousand Villages, <www.tenthousandvillages.com>, 717-859-8100

Valley Farm's Adopt an Apple Tree, <www.desertsweetorganics.com>,
(815) 432-3719

Volunteer Match, <www.volunteermatch.org>

Memberships also make great gifts:

Better World Club, <www.betterworldclub.com>, 866-304-7540

Honeymoon and Wedding Travel

Centers for Disease Control, <www.cdc.gov>

Cruise Junkie, <www.cruisejunkie.com>

Eco-travel section of RedJellyfish.com, <www.redjellyfish.com>,
888-222-5008

Green Earth Travel, <www.vegtravel.com>, 888-2GO-VEGE

Green Maps, <www.greenmap.org>

Planeta, <www.planeta.com>

Responsible Travel, <www.responsibletravel.com>

The International Ecotourism Society, <www.ecotourism.org>,
802-651-9818

Travel section of Gaiam.com, <www.gaiam.com>, 877-989-6321

Transportation

Clean Car Campaign, <www.cleancarcampaign.org>,
202-387-3500

EV Rental, <www.evrental.com>, 877-EV-RENTAL

Greener Cars, <www.greenercars.com>

Zip Car, <www.zipcar.com>, 866-4ZIPCAR

Trips and Tours

Adventure Center, <www.adventure-center.com>, 800-228-8747

Adventure Tours Vietnam, <www.adventure-tours-vietnam.com>,
866-663-9484

Cross Cultural Solutions, <www.crossculturalsolutions.org>

Earthwatch Institute, <www.earthwatch.org>

Habitat for Humanity's Global Village Trips, <www.habitat.org/GV>

Lindblad Expeditions, World Wildlife Fund, <www.expeditions.com>,
800-397-3348

REI Adventures, <www.rei.com/adventures>, 800-622-2236

The American Hiking Society, <www.americanhiking.org>

The Sierra Club Outing Program, <www.sierraclub.org/outings/>, 415-977-5522

Accommodations

Brewery Gulch Inn, <www.brewerygulchinn.com>

CERES Green Hotel Initiative, <www.ceres.org/our_work/ghi.htm>

Co-op America's National Green Pages, <www.greenpages.org>

Green Globe 21, <www.greenglobe21.com>

Green Hotels Association, <www.greenhotels.com>, 713-789-9786

Green Seal's Environmental Lodging Standards, <www.greenseal.org/standards/lodgingproperties.htm>, 202-872-6400

Maho Bay Resorts, St. John, US Virgin Islands, <www.maho.org>, 800-392-9004

National Parks Service, <www.nps.gov>

Sheraton Rittenhouse Square Hotel, Philadelphia, PA <www.sheratonphiladelphia.com>, 215-546-9400

The Greener Lodging Directory, <www.greenerlodging.com>

Travel Organic, <www.travelorganic.com>

Socially Responsible Investing

Green Money Journal, <www.greenmoney.com>

Investor Responsibility Research Center, <www.irrc.org>

Money section of RedJellyfish.com, <www.redjellyfish.com/in-hub.html>

Natural Investment Services, Inc., <www.naturalinvesting.com>

Shareholder Action Network,<www.shareholderaction.org>

Social Funds, <www.socialfunds.com>

Social Investment Forum, <www.socialinvest.org>

Socially Responsible Investing on ENN (Environmental News Network), <www.enn.com/sri>

SRI World Group, <www.sriworld.com>

A Healthy Eco-Home

All Organic Links, <www.allorganiclinks.com>

American Community Garden Association, <www.communitygarden.org>

Bee Natural, <www.beenatural.com>

Earth 911, <www.earth911.org>

Earth-Friendly Products, <www.ecos.com>, 800-335-ECOS

Eco-Friendly Flooring, <www.ecofriendlyflooring.com>

Eco-Labels, <www.eco-labels.org>

Environmental Home Center, <www.environmentalhomecenter.com>

Find Organic Cotton, <www.findorganiccotton.org>

Gaiam, <www.gaiam.com>

Grassroots Recycling Network, <www.grrn.org>, 706-613-7121

Green Guerillas NYC, <www.greenguerillas.org>

Guide to Environmentally Preferable Purchasing, Center for a New American
    Dream, <www.newdream.org/thedream/buygreen>

HealtheHouse, Children's Health Environmental Coalition,
    <www.checnet.org/HealtheHouse>

Healthy Home, <www.healthyhome.com>

Jenni Originals, <www.jennioriginals.com>

Marcal, <www.marcalpaper.com>, 201-796-4000

National Recycling Coalition, <www.nrc-recycle.org>

NSF International Consumer Information, <www.nsfconsumer.org>

Pacifica Candles, <www.pacificacandles.com>

Real Goods, <www.realgoods.com>

Seventh Generation, <www.seventhgeneration.com>

Smart Home Buy, <www.smarthomebuy.com>

The New York City Compost Project, <www.nyccompost.org>

United Health Foundation, <www.unitedhealthfoundation.org>

US Department of Energy, Consumer Energy Information,
    <www.eere.energy.gov/consumerinfo>

Way Out Wax, <www.wayoutwax.com>

Wolverton Environmental, <www.wolvertonenvironmental.com>

Working Assets: phone service, <www.workingassets.com>, 800-788-8588

Eating for Health and Happiness

America's Second Harvest, <www.secondharvest.org>

California Certified Organic Farmers' Organic Directory,
    <www.ccof.org/directory.html>

Center for Science in the Public Interest, <www.cspinet.org>

Chicago's Green City Market, <www.chicagogreencitymarket.org>

Community Alliance with Family Farmers, <www.caff.org>, 530-756-8518

Diamond Organics, <www.diamondorganics.com>

Ecofish, <www.ecofish.com>

Equal Exchange coffee, <www.equalexchange.com>

Food/Wine section of <www.RedJellyfish.com>

Global Exchange, <www.globalexchange.org>

Green Restaurant Association, <www.dinegreen.com>

Greenmarket Farmers' Market, Council on the Environment of New York City,
    <www.cenyc.org>, 212-477-3220

Greenpeace True Food Network, <www.truefoodnow.org>

Jaffe Brothers Natural Foods, <www.organicfruitsandnuts.com>

Local Harvest, <www.localharvest.org>

New York State Harvest Calendar,
    <www.agmkt.state.ny.us/HarvestCalendar.html>

O'Naturals, <www.onaturals.com>

Organic Farming Research Association, <www.ofra.org>

Organic Provisions, <www.orgfood.com>

Organic Vintners, <www.organicvintners.com>

Passion Fish, <www.passionfish.org>

Seafood Watch List, Monterey Bay Aquarium,
    <www.mbayaq.org/cr/seafoodwatch.asp>

Slow Food, <www.slowfood.com>

The Audubon Society, <www.audubon.org>

The Chefs Collaborative, <www.chefscollaborative.org>

The Rodale Institute, <www.rodaleinstitute.org>, 610-683-1400

USDA National Organic Program, <www.ams.usda.gov/nop>

Whole Foods Markets, <www.wholefoods.com>

Click to Learn

You've clicked as a couple and have probably spent countless hours zooming around the Internet to help you plan your wedding and honeymoon. When you're ready for a break from all that — take a look at the links below. Thanks to our inspirational eco-leaders, whose interviews you'll find throughout this book, we've collected a well-recommended list. During our interviews, we asked each of them to share with us favorite organizations they thought would provide you with some meaningful Internet time.

- Alice Waters, Chez Panisse Restaurant, <www.chezpanisse.com>
- Slow Food <www.slowfood.org>; The Edible Schoolyard Project <www.edibleschoolyard.org>. *Interview in Chapter 1*
- Amy Domini, Domini Social Investments, <www.domini.com>
- The Pesticide Action Network <www.panna.org>; The International Right to Know Campaign <www.irtk.org>. *Interview in Chapter 2*
- Kat James, InformedBeauty.com, <www.informedbeauty.com>
- Organic Consumers Association <www.oca.org>; Union of Concerned Scientists <www.ucsusa.org>; Purefood.org. *Interview in Chapter 3*
- Betsy Taylor, Center for a New American Dream, <www.newdream.org>
- Turn the Tide section of the New Dream web site. *Interview in Chapter 5*
- Barney Feinblum, Organic Vintners, <www.organicvintners.com>. *Interview in Chapter 6*
- Social Venture Network <www.svn.org>. *Interview in Chapter 6*
- Nora Pouillon, Restaurant Nora and Asia Nora, <www.noras.com>. *Interview in Chapter 6*
- Organic Trade Association <www.ota.org>; The Center for Science in the Public Interest <www.cspinet.org>; Environmental Nutrition <www.environmentalnutrition.com>. *Interview in Chapter 6*
- Dave Smith, Organic Bouquet, <www.organicbouquet.com>
- The Mendocino Organic Network, <www.MendocinoOrganicNetwork.com>.
- Ukiah Brewing Company <www.UkiahBrewingCo.com>. *Interview in Chapter 7*
- Gary Hirshberg, Stonyfield Farm, <www.stonyfieldfarm.com>. *Interview in Chapter 9*

PHOTO CREDITS

Our enormous thanks goes to the many talented photographers whose wonderful images throughout this book bring the concept of Organic Weddings to life:

Azariah Aker, Brattleboro, VT
Tel. 802-254-2309
Email: azaker20@hotmail.com
Pages: 6, 7, 47 ©Azariah Aker

John Arcara Photography, Red Bank, NJ
Tel. 732-299-9537
Web: www.johnarcara.com, Email:
john@johnarcara.com
Pages: 18, 41, color plates: 5 and 7 ©John
Arcara

Randy Barnes, Ophir, CO
Tel. 970-728-3544
Web: www.barnesfoto.com,
Email: barnesfoto@yahoo.com
Page: 114 ©Randy Barnes

Massimo Calore, Sarcedo (Vicenza), Italy
Tel. 011.39.0445.884124
Email: massimocalore@tiscalinet.it
Pages: 93, color plate 4-Bottom ©Massimo
Calore

Geoffrey Cook Studios, Menasha, WI
Tel. 920-969-3944
Web: www.geoffreycookstudios.com,
Email: comphoto@athenet.net
Pages: 1, 49 ©Geoffrey Cook

Hélène Cyr, Victoria, B.C., Canada
Tel. 250-995-8787
Web: www.hcphotos.com, Email:
helene@hcphotos.com
Pages: 45, color plate 1 ©Hélène Cyr

Derek Photographers, Greenwich, CT
Tel. 800-443-3735
Web: www.derekphotographers.com
Page: front cover ©Derek Photographers

Cory Despres Photography, Boston, MA
Tel. 781-233-9110
Web: www.corydespresphotography.com,
Email: cmdespres@attbi.com
Pages: 2, 55, 62, 74, 109, color plate: 8-Top
Right ©Cory Despres

Leslie Elias, Grass Valley, CA
Tel. 530-272-3908
Email: leslieelias@hotmail.com
Pages: 26, 27, 72, 80 ©Leslie Elias

Carlos Esteva, Rio Piedras, Puerto Rico
Tel. 787-758-5062
Email: esteva@coqui.net
Pages: 60, 61, 124, 137 ©Carlos Esteva

Genesis Photography, Mountain View, CA
Tel. 650-967-2301
Web: www.genesisphoto.com, Email:
info@genesisphoto.com
Pages: 51, 52, 96, color plate: 8-Top Left
©Genesis Photography

John Heymann Studios, Somerville, MA
Tel. 617-628-4791
Pages: 154, color plate 2 ©John Heymann

Jim Johnson Photography, Washington,
D.C.
Tel. 202-686-7300 or 800-557-3896
Web: www.picturestorystudio.com,
Email: jimjphoto@aol.com
Page: color plate 6 ©Jim Johnson

Paula Moser, Greenwich, CT
Tel. 917-589-7484 or 203-531-8103
Web: www.paulamoser.com,
Email: photos@paulamoser.com
Page: 102 ©Paula Moser

Northlight Photography, Boise, ID
Tel. 208-336-8603
Pages: 126, color plate 3 ©Northlight
Photography

Alison Pouliot, Stellar Black Visual
Communications, Australia
Tel. 03.5476.4344,
Email: stellar@netcon.net.au
Pages: 17, 83, 91, 134, 140 ©Alison Pouliot

Jon Reis Photography, Ithaca, NY
Tel. 607-272-1966
Web: www.jonreis.com,
Email: jon@jonreis.com
Pages: 4, 25, 43, 71, 78, 99, 104, 105, 131
©Jon Reis

Erika Sidor, Worcester, MA
Tel. 508-929-8659
Web: www.pbase.com/erikajake,
Email: erikasidor@yahoo.com
Pages: 20, 28, 64, 127, color plate 8-Bottom
Left ©Erika Sidor

Michael Weintrob/Groovetography, New
York, NY
Tel. 720-935-6509
Web: www.groovetography.com,
Email: michael@groovetography.com
Page: 57 ©Michael Weintrob

Michael Weschler Photography,
Los Angeles, CA
Tel. 323-463-2002
Web: www.michaelweschler.com,
Email: mw@michaelweschler.com
Page: author photo back cover ©Michael
Weschler

Chuck Waskuch, Stowe, VT
Tel. 802-888-5797
Web: www.cwphoto.com,
Email: chuck@cwphoto.com
Page: 31 ©Chuck Waskuch

Other photo credits:

Page 11 ©Getty Images

Page 32 by Ed Falkowski

Page 95 courtesy of Evergreen Memories

Page 113 by ©Getty Images

Page 117 by ©Getty Images

Page 119 by Brett Dotson

Color plate 4-Top by Dean Smith

Color plate 8-Bottom Right by Rachel
Leising

Alice Waters' photo by Doug Hamilton,
page 8

Amy Domini's photo by Jim Robinette,
page 22

Kat James' photo by William Abranowicz,
page 36

Betsy Taylor's photo by Jennifer Errick,
page 68

Barney Feinblum's photo by Andy Katz,
page 84

Nora Pouillon's photo by Gozen Koshida,
page 88

Dave Smith's photo by Beverly Smith,
page 106

Gary Hirshberg's photo by Stonyfield Farm,
page 156

Custom wedding attire designs by Michelle
Kozin for Organic Weddings can be seen on
pages: 18, 31, 32, 41, 102, 114, 126, 154,
and color plates: 2, 3, 4, 5, 6

Custom invitations by Organic Weddings
can be seen on page 51.

INDEX

INDEX *187*

About the Author

MICHELLE KOZIN is founder and president of Organic Weddings, Inc. (www.organicweddings.com), the only comprehensive source for wedding planning ideas, information, resources and products for couples living healthy, natural lifestyles with regard for environmental issues and social responsibility.

With years of experience in business management, marketing, design and event planning, Michelle founded the company to improve awareness and accessibility to "people- and planet-friendly" living, as well as to conscientious commerce. Through Organic Weddings, she has pioneered and formalized a new opportunity for making purchasing decisions that support stylish living centered on health and sustainability.

An MBA, Michelle previously worked as a change management consultant with Andersen Consulting (now Accenture). The birth of her first child motivated her to make a difference with her career. During the course of her pregnancy, she researched how environmental toxins and other common pollutants are especially dangerous for children. Because of her concerns for the environmental and social problems facing younger generations in the US and around the world, she decided to use her skills, style and creativity to promote a healthier, balanced way of life through environmental and social stewardship. She lives in Massachusetts.

If you have enjoyed *Organic Weddings* you might also enjoy other

BOOKS TO BUILD A NEW SOCIETY

Our books provide positive solutions for people who want to make a difference. We specialize in:

Sustainable Living • Ecological Design and Planning • Natural Building & Appropriate Technology
New Forestry • Environment and Justice • Conscientious Commerce • Progressive Leadership
Educational and Parenting Resources • Resistance and Community • Nonviolence

For a full list of NSP's titles, please call 1-800-567-6772 or check out our web site at:
www.newsociety.com

New Society Publishers

ENVIRONMENTAL BENEFITS STATEMENT

New Society Publishers has chosen to produce this book on 100% recycled paper made with 30% post consumer waste, processed chlorine free.

For every 5,000 books printed, New Society saves the following resources:[1]

11	Trees
978	Pounds of Solid Waste
1,076	Gallons of Water
1,404	Kilowatt Hours of Electricity
1,778	Pounds of Greenhouse Gases
8	Pounds of HAPs, VOCs, and AOX Combined
3	Cubic Yards of Landfill Space

[1]Environmental benefits are calculated based on research done by the Environmental Defense Fund and other members of the Paper Task Force who study the environmental impacts of the paper industry.

For more information on this environmental benefits statement, or to inquire about environmentally friendly papers, please contact New Leaf Paper – info@newleafpaper.com Tel: 888 • 989 • 5323.

NEW SOCIETY PUBLISHERS